RICHARD

The
OVERLOOKED
LETTERS

The Kennedy Assassination

outskirtspress

DENVER, COLORADO

Outskirts Press, Inc.
http://www.outskirtspress.com

Paperback ISBN: 978-1-4787-0402-7
Hardback ISBN; 978-1-4787-0348-8

Library of Congress Control Number: 2013914542

Outskirts Press and the "OP" logo are trademarks belonging to Outskirts Press, Inc.

PRINTED IN THE UNITED STATES OF AMERICA

Preface

My purpose for writing this historical treatise is to present a theory on a possible motive for the assassination of President John F. Kennedy on November 22, 1963. This motive, which I detail in the following chapters, is one that was considered and rejected by the Warren Commission that investigated the assassination of the President.

I briefly explored several other conspiracy theories considered and also rejected by the Warren Commission. One such theory was that Lee Harvey Oswald and Jack Ruby (Oswald's killer) knew each other prior to President Kennedy's assassination. I note that in 1992 the Dallas Police Department released some heretofore secret files that may relate to an Oswald/Ruby connection. Research into these documents is not part of this book, however. My conclusions center on the role of Lee Harvey Oswald and his connections to the former Soviet Union.

I do not in any aspect want to imply that Russian President Vladimir Putin, a former KGB officer, or any member of the current Russian government was involved in a conspiracy to assassinate President Kennedy. President Putin, at the time of the Kennedy assassination, was eleven years old.

In this 50th Anniversary year of President Kennedy assassination, I dedicate this historical study to my alma mater: The College of Arts and Sciences, History Department, American University, Washington, D.C.

Lastly, I am most appreciative to Mary Alice Davidson, principal at Davidson Communications, for her editorial assistance.

Richard F. Cross
Loudon, Tennessee
September 2013

Prologue

Along with most Americans who were alive when it happened, I vividly remember where I was and what I was doing at 11:40 am (CST) on November 22, 1963, when President John F. Kennedy was assassinated in Dallas, Texas. I was chief security officer for the Institute of Defense Analysis and was parking my car at the Military District of Washington headquarters in southeast Washington, D.C., when I heard the announcement of the shooting.

I had a personal connection to President Kennedy. On November 28, 1961, the President visited the new Central Intelligence Agency (CIA) headquarters in Langley, VA, and presented the National Security Medal to CIA Director Allen Dulles. I was a member of the agency's physical security team assigned to assist the U.S. Secret Service during the President's visit. My duty station was in the large main entrance lobby; I was armed and standing with Secret Service agents next to a wall about fifty feet from the President. My job was to assist the Secret Service agents in their movement around the headquarters and to respond to any emergency as directed by the President's protective team. I was most honored to be one of only a few CIA employees to witness this historic event as we observed the President's speech and Director Dulles's acceptance of the medal.

Because I had seen, heard, and protected President Kennedy two years earlier, I was particularly shaken by his assassination. In light of my security training, I closely followed the resulting arrests and investigations. However, despite exhaustive government and law enforcement research into that fatal day, I have always had a nagging feeling that there was more to the story—that the events and players that intersected that day were on a trajectory that had its roots in murky but interconnected scenarios.

My Visit to Dallas

In September 1998, I went to the place of the shooting attack at Dealey Plaza and walked to the top of the grassy hill. I strolled around the plaza, toured the Texas School Book Depository, and peered through the sixth floor window where the Warren Commission concluded Lee Harvey Oswald fired the three fatal rifle shots that killed President Kennedy.

As I stood at this window gazing down to the approximate location of the President's vehicle, I found it difficult to accept the Commission's view that Oswald was the sole planner and assassin. This visit to Dallas confirmed my suspicions. To test my hypothesis, I purchased and poured through an abridged version of the Warren Commission report shortly after it was published in 1964 by the Associated Press.

During the ensuing fifty years since that most tragic event in America's history, I have frequently reflected on—and now challenge—the Commission's conclusion that found no evidence that either Lee Harvey Oswald or his assassin, Jack Ruby, was part of any conspiracy, domestic or foreign, to assassinate President Kennedy.[1]

Evidence in the Overlooked Letters

As I studied the Warren Commission's report and voluminous exhibits, I took a fresh look at various letters written by Oswald before the assassination. Three letters in particular were troubling to me.

Consider, for instance, the Warren Commission's report of a letter from Oswald to his brother, Robert, sent from Minsk, USSR. This letter confirms that Oswald saw Francis Gary Powers prior to Powers' release from a Soviet prison and his return to the United States. Powers was the CIA U-2 pilot whose plane was shot down on a secret flight over the Soviet Union on May 1, 1960; he was convicted by the Soviets of a crime against their union and jailed. This piece of evidence is an important primary resource for my conclusions (see Chapter 4).

Also of interest were the letters Oswald wrote to the U. S. Embassy in Moscow after he had defected to the Soviet Union in 1959. At the time of his requests, Oswald was classified as a "stateless person" by the Soviet government and was living in Minsk. The letters expressed his desire to repatriate to the United States. But Oswald wrote on several occasions that he was unable to travel because he did not have a passport as a stateless person. Mysteriously, however, the final written plea was postmarked from Moscow, suggesting that he had Soviet, even KGB, help in getting back to the United States (see Chapter 7).

Finally, once back in the U.S., Oswald traveled to Mexico City just weeks before the actual assassination. On this trip, he wrote letters to Cuban and Soviet officials in Mexico seeking entry into Cuba to see Fidel Castro. When those attempts were thwarted, he penned a letter to the Soviet Embassy in Washington, D.C., a letter he drafted numerous times. A closer look at the original and drafts that survived reveal a coded attempt, in my view, to inform his KGB handlers that his inability to reach Cuba was a mistake and that he had failed in that mission (see Chapter 8).

Conclusions

Drawing on my lifetime experiences in assignments with the CIA, U.S. Army, private sector corporate security, ASIS International leadership, as well as my Dallas visit and consultations with Russians following the 1991 downfall of the USSR, I now postulate the following theory:

Prior to the Kennedy assassination, Lee Harvey Oswald was a secret undercover operative under control of the Soviet KGB. Oswald became a KGB agent while he was on active duty with the U.S. Marine Corps in Atsugi, Japan, during 1957 and remained under KGB control as an alleged American defector in Minsk, USSR. Upon his return to the United States in 1962, Oswald continued to be a Soviet intelligence secret agent under the control of the KGB.

In the following chapters, my research into and assumptions on the assassination are related in detail. My investigative findings and observations support the theory that the Soviet Union and the KGB could have been active participants in planning the assassination of President Kennedy.

In the Postscript, I relate my experiences when meeting with and providing bank security training to former KGB officers from 1991-1995 following the break-up of the former Soviet Union. Also, following my January 1995 speech in Moscow, I revisit an encounter with an attendee where I confirmed my belief of a Soviet intelligence capability in Japan during the 1950s.

Contents

1

The Assassination and Its Aftermath

On Friday, November 22, 1963, President John F. Kennedy, Mrs. Kennedy, and their party arrived at Love Field, Dallas, Texas. They had just completed the first day of a trip planned five months before by the President, Vice President Lyndon B. Johnson, and John B. Connally, Jr., governor of Texas. A motorcade through downtown Dallas was on the itinerary.[2]

The Presidential Motorcade

By midmorning, rain and overcast skies gave way to bright sunshine as Air Force One touched down. Governor and Mrs. Connally and Senator Ralph W. Yarborough flew with the Kennedys from Fort Worth. Vice President Johnson's airplane, Air Force Two, had previously arrived at Love Field, and the Johnsons were in the receiving line waiting to greet the President and First Lady.[3]

After a welcome from the Dallas reception committee, President and Mrs. Kennedy walked along a chain-link fence greeting a large crowd of spectators. Secret Service agents formed a cordon to keep the press and photographers from impeding the Kennedys and scanned the crowd for threatening movements. Dallas police stood at intervals along the fence, and Dallas plainclothes officers mixed in the crowd. Vice President and Mrs. Johnson followed, guarded by four members of the vice presidential detail. Approximately ten minutes after their arrival at Love Field, President and Mrs. Kennedy began their motorcade.[4]

Commission Exhibit No. 697

Best possible image.

Commission Exhibit 263

Best possible image.

President Kennedy's motorcade in Dallas before
and immediately after the shooting.

Previously, on November 8th, the Secret Service was told that forty-five minutes had been allotted for the motorcade to proceed from Love Field to a luncheon in the President's honor planned by Dallas business and civic leaders. After considering several facilities and their potential security problems, the Trade Mart was chosen as the luncheon site. By November 18th, the route was approved by the local host committee and White House representatives and was publicized in the local papers the next day. The advance publicity made it clear that the motorcade would leave Main Street and pass the intersection of Elm and Houston Streets as it proceeded to the Trade Mart by way of the Stemmons Freeway.

The motorcade left Love Field shortly after 11:50 am and drove through residential neighborhoods, stopping twice at the President's request to greet well-wishers among the friendly crowds. As the motorcade reached Main Street, a principal east-west artery in downtown Dallas, the welcome became tumultuous. At the extreme west end of Main Street the motorcade turned right on Houston Street and proceeded north for one block to make a left turn on Elm Street, the most direct and convenient approach to the Stemmons Freeway and the Trade Mart. As the President's car approached the intersection of Houston and Elm Streets, directly ahead on the intersection's northwest corner was a seven-story orange brick warehouse and office building called the Texas School Book Depository.

The President's car made a sharp turn onto Elm Street. At a speed of about eleven miles per hour, it started down the gradual descent toward a railroad overpass that would lead them to the Stemmons Freeway. The front of the Texas School Book Depository was now on the President's right, and he waved to the crowd assembled there as the motorcade passed the building. Dealey Plaza, across the street, was an open, landscaped grassy knoll, which marked the western end of downtown Dallas. Seconds later, shots resounded in rapid succession. The President's hands moved to his neck. He appeared to stiffen momentarily and lurch slightly forward in his seat. He had been shot.

The Death of President Kennedy

The President's car proceeded at high speed to Parkland Memorial Hospital, four miles away. At Parkland, the President was immediately treated by a team of physicians who had been alerted for the President's arrival by the Dallas police traveling with the motorcade. The doctors noted irregular breathing and a possible heartbeat, although they could not detect a pulse. They observed an extensive wound in the President's head and a small wound approximately one-fourth inch in diameter in the lower third of his neck. In an effort to facilitate breathing, the physicians performed a tracheotomy by enlarging the throat wound and inserting a tube. At 1:00 pm, after all heart activity ceased and the Last Rites were administered by a priest, President Kennedy was pronounced dead.[5]

While the team of doctors at Parkland Hospital tried desperately to save the life of the President, Mrs. Kennedy alternated between watching them and waiting outside. After the President was pronounced dead, presidential staff member Kenneth O'Donnell tried to persuade Mrs. Kennedy to leave the area, but she refused; she intended to stay with her husband. A casket was obtained and the President's body was prepared for removal.

Before the body could be taken from the hospital, two Dallas officials informed the president's staff that the body could not be removed from the city until an autopsy was performed. Despite the protests of these officials, the casket was wheeled out of the hospital, placed in an ambulance, and transported to the airport shortly after 2:00 pm. At approximately 2:15 pm, the casket was loaded, with some difficulty because of the narrow airplane door, onto the rear of the Air Force One where seats had been removed to make room. Concerned that the local officials might try to prevent the plane's departure, O'Donnell asked the pilot to take off immediately. He was informed that takeoff would be delayed until Vice President Johnson was sworn in.[6]

Upon learning of the President's death, Vice President Johnson left Parkland Hospital under close guard and proceeded to the presidential plane at Love Field. Mrs. Kennedy, accompanying her husband's body, boarded the plane shortly thereafter. At 2:38 pm, in the central compartment of the plane, Lyndon B. Johnson was sworn in as the 36th

President of the United States by Federal District Court Judge Sarah T. Hughes.[7]

The Texas Book Depository Building

At the scene of the shooting, there was evident confusion at the outset concerning the point of origin of the shots. Witnesses differed in their accounts of the direction from which the sound of the shots emanated. Within a few minutes, however, attention centered on the Texas School Book Depository building as the source of the shots. The building was occupied by a private corporation, the Texas School Book Depository Company, which distributed textbooks from several publishers and leased space to the publishers and their employees. Others who frequented the building included a fifteen-person warehousing crew, employees of the company.

Several eyewitnesses in front of the Depository reported that they saw a rifle being fired from a window in the southeast corner of the sixth floor. One eyewitness who had been watching the motorcade from Elm Street directly opposite and facing the building told a police officer that he had seen a slender man, about 5 feet 10 inches in his early thirties, take deliberate aim from the sixth floor corner window and fire a rifle in the direction of the President's car.

The Dallas police entered the Depository building and encountered Lee Harvey Oswald, who had started working there on October 16th. Oswald was seen passing through the second floor offices. In his hand was a full Coke bottle, which he had purchased from a vending machine in the lunchroom. He was walking toward the front of the building where a passenger elevator and a short flight of stairs lead to the main entrance on the first floor.

The Shooting of Patrolman Tippit

Approximately seven minutes later, at about 12:40 pm, Oswald boarded a bus on Elm Street seven short blocks east of the Depository. The bus was traveling west toward the very building from which Oswald had come. Its route traversed through the Oak Cliff section in southwest Dallas, where it would pass seven blocks east of the rooming house in which Oswald was living. On the bus was one of Oswald's former landladies who immediately recognized him. Oswald stayed on the bus approximately three or four minutes, during which time it proceeded only two blocks because of the traffic jam created by the motorcade and the assassination. Oswald then left the bus.

A few minutes later, Oswald entered a vacant taxi four blocks away and asked the driver to take him to a point on North Beckley Avenue several blocks beyond his rooming house. The trip required five or six minutes. At about 1:00 pm, Oswald arrived at his rooming house. The housekeeper was surprised to see Oswald at midday and remarked to him that he seemed to be in quite a hurry. He made no reply. A few minutes later Oswald emerged from his room, zipped up his jacket, and rushed out of the house.

Approximately forty-five minutes after the Kennedy assassination, Dallas Police Patrolman J. D. Tippit was shot near the intersection of 10th Street and Patton Avenue, about nine-tenths of a mile from Oswald's rooming house. At the time of the assassination, Tippit was alone in his patrol car, a routine practice for most police patrol officers at this time of day. He had been ordered by radio at 12:45 pm to proceed to the central Oak Cliff area as part of a concentration of patrol cars around the center of the city following the assassination.

At around 1:15 pm, Tippit was driving slowly in an easterly direction on 10th Street in Oak Cliff. About one hundred feet past the intersection of 10th Street and Patton Avenue, Tippit pulled up alongside a man walking in the same direction. The man met the general description of the suspect wanted in connection with the assassination. He walked over to Tippit's car, rested his arms on passenger door, and apparently exchanged words with Tippit through the window. Tippit opened the driver's side door and started to walk around the front of his car. As he reached the front wheel, the man on the sidewalk drew a revolver and fired several shots in rapid succession, hitting Tippit four times and killing him instantly. A witness promptly reported the shooting to police headquarters, using the radio in Tippit's car.

Oswald's Arrest

Another witness observed the gunman going back toward Patton Avenue, removing the empty cartridge cases from the gun as he went and turning left or south. Other witnesses saw the suspect, Oswald, enter the Texas Theatre, a motion picture house about sixty feet away, without buying a ticket.

A police radio sounded an alarm: "Have information: a suspect just went in the Texas Theatre on West Jefferson." Within minutes the theater was surrounded, and the house lights were turned up. Patrolman M. N. McDonald and several other police officers approached the man. McDonald ordered the man to his feet and heard him say, "Well, it's all over now." The man drew a gun from his waist with one hand and struck the officer with the other. McDonald struck out with his right hand and grabbed the gun with his left hand. After a brief struggle, McDonald and several other police officers, including Detective Paul Bentley, disarmed and handcuffed the suspect and drove him to police headquarters, arriving at approximately 2:00 pm.

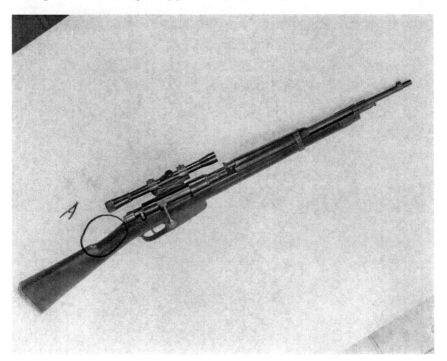

The rifle Oswald used to kill President Kennedy.

Meanwhile, shortly before 1:00 pm, Captain J. Will Fritz, chief of the homicide and robbery bureau of the Dallas Police Department, arrived at the Texas School Book Depository building to take charge of the investigation there. After receiving Oswald's name, address, and general description, Fritz left for police headquarters. He arrived short-ly after 2:00 pm and asked two detectives to pick up the employee who was missing from the Depository. Standing nearby were the po-lice officers who had just arrived with the man arrested in the Texas Theatre. When Fritz mentioned the name of the missing employee, he learned that the man was already in the interrogation room. The miss-ing Depository employee and the suspect who had been apprehended in the Texas Theatre were one and the same—Lee Harvey Oswald.

.

2

The Investigation

An investigation into the facts of a serious national security event, such as President Kennedy's assassination, required the combined resources and modes of operations of numerous federal departments and agencies designated to conduct investigations. After his arrest, Lee Harvey Oswald was investigated or interrogated by the Dallas Police Department, the FBI, the Secret Service, and the U.S. Postal Service.[8] Various departments of the CIA investigated Oswald's movements outside the United States. The Warren Commission gathered evidence from all sectors and heard testimony from both government and civilian witnesses.

Interestingly, my research into the Kennedy assassination failed to produce a record of any interview of Detective Paul Bentley, the arresting officer, by the federal law enforcement agents that pursued the case.[9]

The Federal Bureau Investigation

The secretary of the Department of Justice and the director of the FBI, with a few exceptions, are responsible for investigating crimes—including assassinations, espionage, violence, and white-collar crime—under Title 18 of the United States Code. The FBI director, prior to and following President Kennedy's assassination, was J. Edgar Hoover. The vast majority of investigative activity that led to the conclusions in the 1964 Warren Commission Report was done by FBI agents.

Before 1963, FBI agents probably conducted hundreds of "black bag jobs," or warrantless searches of an individual's home, office, automobile, and other personal affects. These pursuits often included searching a physical premises and photographing documents. Most of the searches, if not all, were done without an attorney general's approval but were authorized by Director Hoover and supervised by his trusted colleague, Associate Director Clyde Tolson. All black bag job reports were personally delivered to either Hoover or Tolson.

The FBI agents who engaged in black bag jobs were trained in lock picking and wiretap installations. During my private sector employment, I confirmed that the FBI used warrantless searches through conversations with retired agents who were friends and business associates, now deceased. In my view, it is probable that FBI black bag job files have been destroyed; yet, it is also possible that some remain hidden inside an FBI vault.

The U.S. Secret Service

At the time of the Kennedy assassination, the Secret Service was under the jurisdiction of the secretary of the U.S. Department of the Treasury. The Presidential Protective Branch of the Secret Service consumed only a small portion of the Service's annual funding. Most resources were directed toward the counterfeiting of U.S. currency, U.S. official checks, and U.S. Treasury securities. The Secret Service also had responsibility for investigating illegal sales of tobacco, alcohol, and firearms. Following President Kennedy's assassination, the Secret Service did an extensive investigation into its security practices for rendering protective services to Presidents and their families, and the Service implemented many enhancements to its Presidential protection program.

The U.S. Postal Service

The U.S. Postal Inspection Service is responsible for enforcing federal statutes that deal with the U.S. Postal Service. Postal inspectors are federal law enforcement agents, and the Office of the Chief Postal Inspector is in Washington, D.C. Regional Postal Inspection offices are located in major U.S. cities, including Dallas, Texas. Postal inspection agents were involved in the interrogation of Lee Harvey Oswald. Questioning centered on the post office boxes that Oswald opened and closed in New Orleans and Dallas, which may have been used to receive and send secret messages to his KGB handlers (see Chapters 6 and 8).

The Central Intelligence Agency

The CIA has no criminal domestic U.S. investigative legislative authority or responsibility for the conduct of criminal investigations. The National Security Act of 1947, however, does require the CIA director to protect intelligence sources and methods from unauthorized disclosure.

John McCone was the CIA director prior to and following President Kennedy's assassination.

Senior Officer James J. Angleton was in charge of the CIA Directorate for Counterintelligence (CI). I believe Angleton and his staff of CI officers would have been involved in any CIA investigation into a possible foreign conspiracy to assassinate President Kennedy.

During my employment at the CIA, the Office of Security maintained a small counterintelligence staff. On occasion, one or more members of the Security CI staff would interface with Angleton, who was generally viewed as having a trusted relationship with FBI Director Hoover. I believe it is possible Angleton had access to highly sensitive FBI intelligence on suspected communists derived from warrantless (black bag) searches that were not available for review by the CIA Office of Security.

The Warren Commission

The President's Commission on the Assassination of President John F. Kennedy was created on November 29, 1963, by President Lyndon Johnson who recognized that people everywhere had a right to a full and truthful exploration of the tragic events. The Commission was composed of the following highly respected individuals: Chief Justice Earl Warren as chairman, U.S. Senators John Sherman Cooper and Richard Russell, U.S. Representatives Hale Boggs and Gerald Ford, former director of the CIA Allan Dulles, and past president of the World Bank John McCloy.[10]

The Commission was deeply aware of its responsibility to provide the American people with an objective view of the facts relating to the assassination. In the introduction, the Commission report states that it "endeavors to appraise the tragedy by the light of reason and the standard of fairness."[11]

The official report consists of several thousand pages and more than three thousand exhibits. The Associated Press published an abridged version in 1964. An introductory note posed numerous questions: Was John Kennedy actually murdered by Lee Harvey Oswald and, if so, had Oswald acted alone? Had Jack Ruby known Oswald? Were they somehow knowing or unknowing parts of the same conspiracy, one to kill the President and the other to silence the killer? "Were we to believe…that a sullen little man for his own twisted reasons, could kill a President and then while in police custody, himself be killed by another little man with his twisted reasons?"

In the introduction to *The Warren Report: The Official Report on the Assassination of President Kennedy*, editor Saul Pett, special correspondent with the Associated Press, writes that the answers can be found in the pages of the report, but adds, "Will history be fully content with the answers? History is rarely content in these matters."[12]

In his forward to the 2004 book, *A Presidential Legacy and the Warren Commission*, President Gerald Ford points out that the report's twenty-six volumes "exhaustively cover the bases for its conclusions, which have yet to be proved wrong" although, he admits they could be in the future. Nonetheless, penned the President, "this report has withstood forty years of constant inquisition."[13]

3

The CIA's U-2 Program

Following my visit to Dallas in 1998, I realized I was not content with the answers reported by the Warren Commission about the assassination of President John F. Kennedy in 1963 and Lee Harvey Oswald's involvement in it. I began sifting through the Warren Commission report and its exhibits and weighed them against my recollections of what I saw, heard, and read while on a Central Intelligence Agency (CIA) deployment to Japan.[14]

In April, 1952, I became a member of the CIA Office of Security. Shortly after reporting for duty at the CIA headquarters in Washington, D.C., I was selected for a two-year assignment in Tokyo, Japan. The CIA, during the Korean War, made an arrangement with the U.S. Department of Defense, which allowed eligible agency employees who agreed to serve overseas for two or more years to be classified as medically ineligible for the draft (4F). Upon returning to the U.S., employees in the program further agreed to enlist in the army for two years, be discharged after six months of active duty service, and then serve seven and one-half years in the reserves. These reservists were not required to attend monthly meetings or be deployed for annual training. I agreed to these terms and began training for my security assignment to Tokyo, Japan, in January 1953.

My CIA Assignment to Tokyo, Japan

During my two-year deployment to Tokyo, I would occasionally visit two CIA bases that reported to the Chief of Station. One base was at the Atsugi Naval Air Station approximately twenty miles from Tokyo. As part of its hidden past, Atsugi was the site for the CIA base that housed the aircraft used in the secret U-2 program. On November 26, 1954, CIA Director Allen Dulles told his special assistant, Richard Bissell, that President Eisenhower had just approved the U-2 project and placed Bissell in charge.

During the latter months of 1954, I saw a Lockheed CL-282 aircraft, the predecessor to the U-2, parked on the Atsugi tarmac. It was a very unusual looking aircraft with exceptionally long wings, with landing wheels and an airplane design that I had never seen before. Upon questioning the plane's crew members, I was told the aircraft was being used for weather reconnaissance by the Air Force. In my current assignment, I was not cleared by the CIA for involvement in the U-2 program, so I had no need to know any details.

Post World War II Intelligence on the Soviet Union

At the conclusion of World War II, following the American bombing of Hiroshima and Nagasaki, Japan, atomic bomb research continued in England, France, and the USSR. Soviet Premier Stalin concluded that American and Western European dominance of nuclear weapons were a threat to the goal of spreading Communism worldwide. Stalin undertook an accelerated, highly secret program to develop an atomic bomb and missile delivery system. By 1949, the Soviet Union and the states of Eastern Europe had been effectively cut off from the outside world, permitting the Soviets to produce military weapons in the utmost secrecy.

During this post-war period, American intelligence agencies' ability to acquire creditable information about the Soviet Union's atomic bomb development and delivery capabilities from either human sources or internal Soviet documents was difficult since the nation was closed to the West. The United States government urgently needed relevant intelligence information to access the Soviet military's ability to launch a strike toward the U.S. The U-2 program, with its ability to take photographs during overflights of the Soviet Union and Eastern European nations, was proposed to and accepted by President Eisenhower on November 23, 1954.

First U-2 Overflights

On April 29, 1955, Special Assistant Bissell entered into an agreement with the Air Force and Navy (which at that time was also interested in the U-2) in which the departments agreed that the CIA would assume primary responsibility for all security under the CIA Office of Security. This oversight included handling security clearances and the physical security measures for the various contractors manufacturing the aircraft's parts and surveillance cameras.

In June 1956, the first operational flight of a U-2 took place over Poland and East Germany. The photographs were considered to be of good quality. The first U-2 flight from Wiesbaden, West Germany, over the Soviet Union occurred on July 4, 1956. This mission took the U-2 over Leningrad and the Soviet Baltic states. After the successful flights from Wiesbaden, the CIA turned to the Navy and secured permission for U-2 Detachment C to use the Naval Air Station at Atsugi, Japan. U-2 overflights flights from Atsugi began in June 1957.

According to the Warren Commission report, U-2 overflight operations at Atsugi actually commenced in the summer of 1956. This first CIA U-2 detachment at Atsugi was known publicly as the 1st Weather Reconnaissance Squadron, Provisional. The "provisional" designation gave the U-2 detachment greater security because provisional Air Force units did not have to report to a higher headquarters.

By July 4, 1956, the U-2 deployment to Atsugi was complete. Shortly thereafter, the National Advisory Committee on Aeronautics released an unclassified cover story stating a Lockheed-developed aircraft would be flown by the Air Force Air Weather Service to study high-altitude phenomena. I, of course, still believed the CIA's cover story whenever I saw media reporting on the U-2 aircraft at the time.

President Eisenhower and U-2 Operations

President Eisenhower had mixed feelings about U-2 overflights of the Soviet Union. He knew that they could produce extremely valuable intelligence about Soviet capabilities. Yet, on the other hand, he was very aware that the flights brought with them the risk of war. From the beginnings of the U-2 program in 1955, the President resisted attempts by the Air Force to take control of the project from the CIA. He believed, if found to be military aircraft, the flights could be considered an act of war by the Soviets.

One CIA argument that helped him to overcome his fear that the flights would be detected by the Soviets was based on a 1952 study of Soviet World War II vintage radar and supported by a 1955 test of U.S. radars. It re-confirmed that "Maximum Soviet radar detection ranges against the Project aircraft at elevation in excess of 55,000 feet would vary from 20 to 150 miles…however, it is doubtful that the Soviets can achieve consistent tracking of the Project vehicle."[15]

The July 1956 overflights brought a strong protest from the Soviet Union in the form of a note handed to the U.S. Embassy in Moscow. The note stated flights could only be viewed as "intentional and conducted for the purposes of intelligence." The initial U-2 flights flew above 69,000 feet and could be seen only fleetingly by pilots of the Soviet interceptor aircraft. But, when the note reached the White House on July 10, 1956, U-2 Project Director Bissell stopped all U-2 overflights. Thus, at least after July 1956, both the U.S. civilian and Soviet military intelligence agencies were aware that the U-2 flights could be detected at heights greater than 69,000 feet.

The Soviet Union's actions in Hungary during the fall of 1956, along with other events in Eastern Europe, convinced President Eisenhower to authorize renewed U-2 flights over the Soviet Bloc. The first of these flights, in November, 1956, was flown by U-2 pilot Francis Gary Powers. The CIA obtained permission from the Department of the Navy to deploy U-2 Detachment C to the Atsugi Naval Air Station, and U-2 missions from Atsugi commenced in June 1957.

Increasing Concerns about Soviet Long Range Missiles

On August 4, 1957, seven U-2 aircraft flew over the Soviet Union, and these flights were the first to photograph the major Soviet space launch facility east of the Aral Sea. I must assume these U-2 flights over the Soviet's most sensitive military operational base were detected by the Soviets and created an immediate urgency for the Soviet government to find a way to shoot down future U-2 flights over their missile and space launch facility. These successful missions continued until March 1958 when the Soviet Union delivered another vigorous protest to President Eisenhower that caused the President to discontinue all U-2 flights over the Soviet Union. This stoppage lasted until July 1959.

During 1959, President Eisenhower and his President's Science Advisory Committee were most concerned about Soviet advances in missile development and the latter's capability to strike the United States with an atomic bomb. Also, during this period, FBI Director Hoover was becoming alarmed about the spread of Soviet intelligence gathering capabilities on the rapidly developing U.S. missile programs undertaken by President Eisenhower's administration.

While I did not have a security clearance for access to U-2 operational data at first, by early 1959 I had been issued the special clearances to see finished intelligence reporting derived from electronic intercepts and U-2 overflight photographs. At the beginning of 1959, I was assigned on loan to the President's Science Advisory Committee (PSAC) then headed by George Kistiakowsky, PhD, who was appointed by President Eisenhower. At that time, the PSAC was very much engaged in highly top secret research and development relating to our nation's guided missile nuclear delivery systems during the "missile gap" with the Soviet Union.

The PSAC occupied office space on the second floor in the old State Department building (now known as the Eisenhower Executive Office Building) on 17th Street located next to the White House West Wing, which houses a majority of the offices for White House staff.

In addition to my CIA identification, I was issued White House credentials that provided interior parking space for my car as well as access to the Eisenhower Executive Office Building (EEOB) and the White House West Wing. Thus, I had free movement within the White House, except for the President's living quarters. (I now regret that I did not find a reason to visit the West Wing operational area and seek a personal introduction with President Eisenhower.)

My primary duties were to establish protocols and physical safeguards for the protection of the top secret intelligence documents on loan to the PSAC and to facilitate the granting of top secret security clearances to the PSAC staff and consultants. The latter, for the most part, were leading professors at our nation's most prestigious universities. On occasion, I would be asked for input on certain aspects of an ongoing report. At that time, I continued to have the special security clearances needed for access to intelligence reporting derived from National Security Agency intercepts and the CIA photographic air surveillance programs.

Resumption of U-2 Overflights

In the summer of 1959 in the mist of the U.S. and Soviet "missile gap" controversy, President Eisenhower again authorized U-2 flights over the Soviet Union after being assured by the CIA that the Soviets were not aware of the U-2s actual operational flight altitude and that the Soviet military did not possess the capability to shoot down a U-2 while flying over the Soviet Union, even if detected. These overflights continued until May1, 1960 when the U-2 piloted by Francis Gary Powers crashed over the Soviet Union.

4

The U-2 Incident

Francis Gary Powers joined the CIA U-2 program in May 1956. He was selected for Operation GRAND SLAM, which would be the most adventurous overflight to date because it proposed covering much of the Soviet Union. Powers was the program's most experienced pilot, having flown twenty-seven U-2 missions over the Soviet Union and China.[16]

Four hours into the mission, Powers saw an airfield that did not appear on his map. An instant after making a turn and notating the location on his chart, he heard a large boom. Writing about his experience at that time, Powers described the attack on his U-2 as follows: "I was marking down these instrument readings when suddenly, there was a dull 'thump,' the aircraft jerked forward, and a tremendous orange flash hit the cockpit and sky...I said 'My God. I've had it now!' "[17]

The CIA report describing the attack said that four-and-a-half hours into the mission, a Soviet SA-2 surface-to-air missile detonated just behind Powers' U-2 and disabled it at 70,500 feet above the Sverdlovsk area. Powers opened the aircraft canopy, was sucked out of the plane, and fell several thousand feet. His parachute opened automatically and drifted to earth where he was surrounded by Russian farmers and then Soviet officials.

Interestingly, this notorious Powers flight occurred on Sunday May 1, 1960, just six days prior to a previously scheduled meeting between

President Eisenhower and Soviet Premier Nikita Khrushchev. The first mention of the incident from the Soviet Union came on May 5th when Khrushchev announced to a meeting of the Supreme Soviet that a U.S. spy plane had been shot down near Sverdlovsk.

Two days later, Khrushchev confirmed that the U-2 pilot, Powers, was alive and had been apprehended. The Soviets engaged in an elaborate show trial for Powers. It started in Moscow on August 17, 1960, and concluded two days later when Powers was sentenced to ten years "deprivation of liberty." For the first three years, he was to be confined in a Soviet prison, but subsequent events negated that verdict (see *Gary Powers Fate*).

Examining the Evidence

My research reveals two extremely important facts about Francis Gary Powers' pre-trial interrogation and trial questioning, which support a theory that the Soviet Union and the KGB were active participants in planning the assassination of President Kennedy.

Powers' writings during the first day of intensive interrogation in Moscow, on May 3, 1960, noted that five persons were present—a colonel, two majors, a stenographer, and an interpreter. When asked about the U-2's operational altitude, Powers always answered incorrectly, saying it was 68,000 feet. Powers later wrote that he wanted to protect other U-2 pilots who may have been still flying at 70,500 feet. Also, upon questioning as to whether he had ever been stationed at the U-2 base located in Atsugi, Japan, he always answered no.

Three months later, during the August trial, Powers estimated that the audience numbered close to a thousand spectators. Powers was asked again by the court about the altitude the U-2 was flying when hit by the missile, and he again incorrectly responded that it was 68,000 feet. He was also asked again if he had ever been assigned to Atsugi, Japan, and he replied no.

In addition to Soviet officials and members of the international media that witnessed the trial, another observer was there: President Kennedy's assassin, Lee Harvey Oswald. While living and working in Minsk, a city approximately 450 miles from Moscow, Oswald amazingly found a way to see Powers in Moscow.

An Overlooked Letter

According to the Warren Commission report Exhibit 315,[18] Oswald wrote the following on February 15, 1962, from Minsk to his brother Robert:

"I heard over the voice of america [sic] that they released Powers the U 2 spy plane fellow. That's big news where you are I suppose. He seemed to be a nice, bright American-type fellow, when I saw him in Moscow."

How could Lee Harvey Oswald travel to Moscow to become involved in the Powers trial? At the time of the trial, Oswald was listed as "stateless person" (see Chapter 6), according to Soviet Union documentation, and was working in Minsk. Travel by a stateless person living in the Soviet Union required prior Soviet government approval. Oswald admits in an undated letter received by the American Embassy in Moscow, postmarked Minsk, February 5, 1961, that he "cannot leave Minsk without permission" of the Soviet government.

There is no record in the Warren Commission report of the Soviet government's approval of Oswald's travel to Moscow to observe the Powers trial. Powers wrote in memoirs that, after his arrest, he remained in prison until he was taken by his jailers to court for his trial; each day after court, he was immediately returned to his jail cell. It stands to reason that Oswald, without KGB assistance, could not have seen Powers while he was at the trial in Moscow or in prison.

In my view, Oswald's attendance at the Powers' trial raises the following questions:

Was Oswald in Moscow to assist the KGB during Powers' initial interrogation and questioning during the trial? Was Oswald's attendance at the Powers' trial a reward for providing the KGB with classified information about the U-2 operational flight altitude that enabled the Soviet's to shoot down the Powers' U-2 airplane?

Oswald was most certainly aware of the U-2's operating altitude of 70,500 feet (see Chapter 5). As a result, I believe it is conceivable and plausible to conclude that the KGB brought Oswald to Moscow for the Powers interrogation and subsequent trial. Also, I conclude that Oswald was a secret agent of the Soviet KGB intelligence service at the time of the Power's trial and that he, Oswald, remained under KGB control after his return to the United States (see Chapter 7).

Gary Powers' Fate

On the morning of February 10, 1962, at the Berlin Wall, Francis Gary Powers was freed and returned to the United States in exchange for Soviet master spy Rudolf Abel. Powers in his memoirs wrote: "After one year, 9 months, and ten days, I was again a free man."[19]

Powers arrived at Andrews Air Force Base in Maryland outside Washington, D.C. and was greeted by a team of CIA security officers. He was taken to a "safe house" known as Ashford Farms near the Eastern Shore town of Oxford, Maryland, where he was reunited with his wife, Barbara, and his parents. He remained there for debriefings and ultimately a meeting with the media.

Following his debriefings, Powers was taken to the CIA offices in northwest Washington, D.C., where he met former CIA Director Allan Dulles. He had been replaced by President Kennedy, who had appointed John A. McCone as the new CIA director. "Dulles greeted me with a bemused look. We shook hands. He commented wryly that he had heard quite a bit about me. I told him how pleased I was to be back in the United States. He replied he had read the debriefing reports. 'We are proud of what you have done.' "[20]

Powers returned to work briefly at the new CIA headquarters in Langley, Virginia, and assumed duties in the agency's training area. In October 1962, he accepted a position at Lockheed as a U-2 test pilot.

Subsequently, Powers flew a helicopter as a traffic reporter for a Los Angeles radio station. On August 1, 1977, Powers died when his helicopter crashed on the way to an assignment.

5 | Oswald's Marine Corp Service

Pertinent incidents and letters throughout Lee Harvey Oswald's life, particularly while he was a U.S. Marine, support the theory that Oswald was a secret undercover agent under control of the Soviet Union's intelligence service at the time of President Kennedy's assassination. The Warren Commission report contains extensive detail about Lee Harvey Oswald's background and United States Marine Corps service.[21]

Oswald's Early Interest in Communist Beliefs

Oswald started to read Communist literature in January 1954 around age fifteen before leaving New York with his mother who was relocating to New Orleans, Louisiana. Oswald was remembered by those who knew him then as a quiet, solitary boy who made few friends. He was briefly a member of the Civil Air Patrol but had few contacts with other people. He read a lot and started at some point to access Communist literature, which he found at the public library.

While still a teenager, Oswald moved with his mother to Fort Worth, Texas, and wrote a letter to the Socialist Party of America.[22]

Oswald's Marine Corp Career

After he turned seventeen, Lee Harvey Oswald enlisted in the U.S. Marine Corps on October 24, 1956. Two days later, he reported for duty at the Marine Corps Recruit Depot in San Diego, California. He was assigned to the Second Recruit Training Battalion and was trained

October 3, 1956

Dear Sirs;

I am sixteen years of age and would like more information about your youth League, I
would like to know if there is a branch in my area, how to join, ect., I am a Marxist, and
have been studying socialist principles for well over fifteen months I am very interested
your Y.P.S.L.

Sincerely

/s/ Lee Oswald

Oswald's letter to the Socialist Party of America.[23]

in the use of the M-1 rifle. When his company fired for record, he scored
two points above the score necessary to qualify as a "sharpshooter."

After boot camp, Oswald reported to the Naval Air Technical
Training Center at the Naval Air Station in Jacksonville, Florida, where
he attended an Aviation Fundamental School. The basic instruction
included subjects such as basic radar theory, map reading, and air
traffic control procedures. This course required Oswald to deal with
confidential material, and he was granted final clearance up to the confidential level.

Oswald next transferred to Keesler Air Force Base in Biloxi, Mississippi, where he attended the Aircraft Control and Warning Operator Course, which included instruction in aircraft surveillance and the use of radar. He continued to hold a confidential clearance.

In September, 1957, Oswald was assigned to Marine Air Control Squadron No. 1 (MACS-1), Marine Air Group 11, 1st Marine Aircraft Wing, based at Atsugi, Japan, about twenty miles west of Tokyo. Prior to Oswald's arrival at the Atsugi base, the CIA had deployed U-2 Detachment C to the Atsugi Naval Air Station.

Oswald's job at Atsugi was that of a radar operator in a unit that had fewer than one hundred men. The unit's function was to direct aircraft to their targets by radar, communicating with the pilots by radio. The squadron also had the duty of scouting for incoming foreign aircraft, such as straying Russian or Chinese planes, which would be intercepted by American planes.

Oswald's squadron remained at Atsugi, with several short temporary Far East deployments, until it was reassigned to El Toro, California, in November 1958. On December 22, 1958, Oswald was assigned to Marine Air Control Squadron No. 9 (MACS-9) at the Marine Corps Air Station at El Toro, where he had been briefly before he went overseas. He was one of about seven enlisted men and three officers who formed a "radar crew" engaged primarily in aircraft surveillance. This work probably gave him access to certain kinds of classified material, some of which—such as aircraft call signs and radio frequencies—was changed after his defection to the Soviet Union in 1959.

Oswald and Soviet Intelligence

As a Marine, Oswald continued to study Marxism and evidenced a strong conviction as to the correctness of the Marxist doctrine. I believe the Soviet Union had an intelligence capability in Japan prior to and during Oswald's Marine Corps assignment to the Atsugi Naval Air Station.[24] Soviet intelligence most certainly was aware of Oswald's involvement with the U-2s at Atsugi and probably his beliefs supporting the Communist ideology.

As noted in Chapter 4, the Soviet Union was able to detect the U-2 overflights as they occurred; however, it needed to acquire more technical data about U-2 altitude capabilities to be able shoot them down. I must assume obtaining this information was of the highest priority for the KGB. In his position as radar operator while at Atsugi, Oswald had a security clearance that most certainly made him aware of the U-2 operation and the plane's technical capabilities, including the maximum operating altitude of 70,500 feet.

According to the Warren Commission report, Oswald arrived at the American Embassy in Moscow and spoke to consul staff member Richard Snyder on October 31, 1959.[25] Oswald told Snyder that he was there to renounce his American citizenship and that he had applied for Soviet citizenship. Oswald also stated to Snyder that he was a Marxist and that his intent to defect to the Soviet Union had been formed before he was discharged from the Marine Corps. Oswald also admitted that he had voluntarily told Soviet officials information about the Marine Corps and his specialty as a radar operator. This conversation suggests that his decision to defect was made while Oswald was in the Far East in 1957 as a radar operator at the Atsugi Naval Air Station.

Is it possible that Oswald, a Marine private with classified knowledge of the U-2 project, could have been recruited as a secret KGB agent, either knowingly or unknowingly, while on assignment at Atsugi, Japan? I believe the answer to this question is yes.

I conclude that Oswald gave the KGB important information about the U-2's operating altitude, which according to CIA unclassified documents published in 1998 was indeed 70,500 feet. I believe Oswald's disclosure of the U-2's operating altitude of 70,500 feet eventually led to the Soviet Union's ability to disable the U-2 piloted by Francis Gary Powers on May 1, 1960.

Powers, in his memoirs about the CIA's U-2 program, wrote about a possible theory that the CIA was involved somehow in a conspiracy to wreck the forthcoming summit meeting between President Eisenhower and Premier Khrushchev. Powers even remarked on Oswald's Marine Corps service at Atsugi, Japan, and the possibility that Oswald may have given the Soviets valuable information about the U-2s.[26]

Powers also wrote that when the U-2's altitude is referred to as secret, that term is qualified. In addition to those personally involved in U-2 flights, a number of others, by the nature of their duties, had access to this information. This would have included air-traffic controllers and some military radar personnel at bases where U-2s were stationed. Thus, I must assume Oswald was surely knowledgeable of the U-2 flying altitude of 70,500 feet.

The Warren Commission report confirms that Oswald was in touch with communists while at Atsugi. It notes that he may have begun to study Russian when he was stationed in Japan. After he arrived in Moscow in October, 1959, he told several persons that he had been planning his defection for two years. This assertion again suggests that the decision was made while he was in the Far East assigned to the Atsugi Naval Air Station, a factor that was not pursued by the Commission.

Let us assume that the KGB recruited Oswald while he was assigned to the Atsugi Naval Air Station and that he disclosed the U-2's classified maximum operating altitude of 70,500 feet to the KGB. (At that point, Oswald was in violation of the U.S. Espionage Act, which prohibits the disclosure of such information to a foreign nation.)

To make Oswald a more valuable asset, the Soviets needed to train Oswald as a secret undercover agent. To obtain such training, Oswald needed to go to the Soviet Union. Thus, I theorize, Oswald was directed by his Soviet handlers in Atsugi to seek early discharge from the Marines and to secretly prepare for future travel to the Soviet Union.

Oswald's Transfer to the Reserves

At his own request, Oswald was transferred from active duty to the Marine Corps Reserve in September, 1959, while in El Toro, California. His main reason, ostensibly, was to give him more time to care for his mother who had relocated to El Toro and had been injured in a workplace accident.

It seems clear from the various recollections of those who knew him at El Toro that by the time Oswald returned to the United States, he no longer had any spirit for the Marines. The attitudes that had prompted his enlistment as soon as he was eligible were entirely gone, and his attention had turned away from the Marines to what he might do after his discharge.

While waiting for his release, The Warren Commission reported that those who knew him in El Toro, in contrast to his associates in Japan, did not doubt that his thoughts were occupied increasingly with Russia and the Russian way of life. He had studied the Russian language enough by February 25, 1959, to request that he be given a foreign language qualification test; his rating was "poor" in all parts of the test.

On September 4, 1959, the very day he was transferred out of MACS-9 in preparation for his discharge, Oswald applied for a passport at the Superior Court of Santa Ana, California. His application stated that he planned to leave the United States on September 21st to attend the University of Turku in Finland, and to travel in Cuba, the Dominican Republic, England, France, Germany, and the Soviet Union. The passport was routinely issued six days later.

On September 11, 1959, Oswald was released from active duty and transferred to the Marine Corps Reserve.

Best possible image.

Oswald's U.S. passport.

WARNING—ALTERATION OR MUTILATION OF ENTRIES IS PROHIBITED

DESCRIPTIVE DATA   SEE PAGE XXX 6 AND 15

NAME			
LEE HARVEY OSWALD			

WIFE			
X X X			

MINORS			
X X X	SEE PAGE -14		

HEIGHT	HAIR	EYES	VISIBLE MARKS
5 ft. 11 in.	BROWN	GREY	X X X

BIRTHPLACE	
NEW ORLEANS, LA.	

BIRTH DATE	OCCUPATION
OCT. 18, 1939	SHIPPING EXPORT AGENT

ISSUE DATE	SIGNATURE OF BEARER
SEPT. 10, 1959	

THIS PASSPORT IS NOT VALID UNLESS SIGNED BY
THE PERSON TO WHOM IT HAS BEEN ISSUED

I, the undersigned, Secretary of State of the United States of America, hereby request all whom it may concern to permit safely and freely to pass, and in case of need to give all lawful aid and protection to the above named citizen(s) of the United States.

Given under my hand and the seal of the Department of State.

Christian A. Herter

Best possible image.

6

Oswald Defects
to the Soviet Union

Lee Harvey Oswald was released from active duty with the U. S. Marine Corps in September, 1959, as a private.[27] At that time, a Marine Corps private's base monthly salary was $83.30. Oswald's monthly pay as a private with more than two years of service, according to my research, would have been $105.00. Warren Commission records show that Oswald served briefly as a private first-class, his highest rank, with a pay grade of E-3, yielding a monthly salary of $124.00. Oswald's total time in the active duty Marine Corps was twenty-two months plus one week. Using a most favorable calculation of $124.00 x 22, his total pay while on active duty would not have exceeded $2,728.00.

Oswald arrived in Moscow on October 16, 1959. According to the Warren Commission, Oswald told an American reporter in Moscow a month later that he had saved $1,500 while in the Marines and implied this money was used to pay for his travel to Moscow.

I served in the U.S. Army in 1955 and received similar pay as an enlisted private. I find it incomprehensible that Oswald saved an average of approximately $68.00 from his monthly pay that ranged from $83.20 to $124.00 during his twenty-two months in the Marine Corps. The Warren Commission notes that while there is no proof that Oswald saved $1,500, as he claimed, it would have taken considerable discipline to save whatever amount was required to finance his defection out of the salary of a low ranking enlisted man.

Did agents of the Soviet Union contribute monies to Oswald prior to his travel from New Orleans to Moscow in September 1959? I believe the answer to this question is yes.

Oswald's Travel to and Arrival in Moscow

Immediately following his release from Marine Corps active duty in early September 1959, Oswald applied for his first civilian U.S. passport. His application stated that he planned to leave the United States and travel to Europe. On September 17, 1959, Oswald booked passage from New Orleans, Louisiana, to Le Havre, France, on a freighter, the SS *Marion Lykes*, scheduled to sail the next day. Oswald paid $220.75 for his ticket and checked into the Liberty Hotel. The freighter actually sailed from New Orleans on September 20th.

In a letter to his mother posted just prior to his departure, Oswald states he did not tell her of his plans because she could not be expected to understand and his values were different from hers. Oswald disembarked from the *Marion Lykes* in Le Havre on October 8th and left for England. A day later, he flew to Helsinki.

In light of the rapid way in which he made connections throughout his entire trip, Oswald probably applied for his Soviet Union visa on October 12th. On October 14th, he was issued Soviet Tourist Visa No. 403339, valid for one six-day visit in the USSR. He left Helsinki on a train destined for Moscow on October 15th.

The visa process was exceptionally quick and inconsistent with the time normally needed to obtain a visa to Moscow. The U.S. Department of State advised the Warren Commission that, according to its information, in 1959 it usually took an American tourist in Helsinki one to two weeks to obtain a visa to Moscow. Thus, it appears that Oswald was given special treatment by the Soviet Union in granting his visa in just two days.

Oswald arrived in Moscow on October 16, 1959. He was greeted at the railroad station by a representative from the Soviet Intourist office and was taken to the Hotel Berlin where he registered as a student. That same day he met Rima Shirokova, an Intourist guide who was assigned to him. Oswald told Shirokova he wanted to become a citizen of the Soviet Union. She passed on this request to the Ministry of Internal

Affairs, which asked Oswald to prepare a letter stating his intention; he mailed the letter the same day.

On October 19th, Oswald met with Lev Setyayec, a reporter with Radio Moscow who was probably acting for the KGB. Setyayec ostensibly was seeking statements from American tourists about their impressions of Moscow. The Warren Commission, however, opined that the Setyayec interview with Oswald may have been an attempt by the KGB to assess Oswald. The Commission also noted that it was aware that many of the Soviet officials that Oswald came in contact with during his stay in the Soviet Union were employees of the KGB.

On October 31, 1959, Oswald went to the American Embassy and declared his intention to "dissolve his American Citizenship. Again, in a November 3, 1959, letter to the Moscow Embassy, Oswald memorialized his intent to defect to the USSR: "I, Lee Harvey Oswald, do hereby request that my present United States citizenship be revoked.[28] For the rest of the year, according to his diary, Oswald remained in his hotel room eight hours a day studying Russian taught by his Intourist guides.

Oswald Sent to Minsk

On January 4, 1959, Oswald was summoned to the Soviet Passport Office and given an identity document for "stateless persons." He was told he was being sent to Minsk, an industrial city located about 450 miles southwest of Moscow. He was directed to a government agency, the Soviet Red Cross, which gave him 5,000 rubles (about $500 at the official exchange rate). He used 2,200 rubles to pay his hotel bill and 150 rubles to purchase a railroad ticket to Minsk.

Oswald arrived in Minsk on January 7th and was met by two Soviet Red Cross workers who took him to the Hotel Minsk where two English-speaking Intourist employees were waiting for him. The next day he met the "mayor" who welcomed him and promised him a rent-free apartment.

In his "Historic Diary," Oswald admits the monies he received from the Soviet Red Cross were not from that group; the funds actually came from the Soviet government. I must assume the governmental agency was the KGB.

According to his diary and documents received from the Soviet government, Oswald resided in Minsk from January, 1960, until June, 1962, which would place him there during the Francis Gary Powers arrest and subsequent trial (May and August 1960). However, Oswald's life in Minsk is largely unknown. The primary sources of information are Oswald's own writings and the testimony of Marina Oswald given during a 1969 trial. Also, the Warren Commission obtained two photographs that were taken by American tourists in Minsk in August 1961 in which Oswald appears, confirming that Oswald was in Minsk on at least two occasions.

While there, according to his diary, Oswald felt like a rich man. He did not receive free living quarters, as the "mayor" of Minsk presumably promised. But shortly after his arrival, Oswald did receive an apartment, very pleasant by Soviet standards, for which he was required to pay only 60 rubles ($6.00) a month. Oswald considered the apartment "almost rent free."

River in Minsk as seen from Oswald's apartment.

Oswald reported to work at the Belorussian Radio and Television Factory on January 13, 1959 as a "metal worker" with a salary that varied between 700 and 900 rubles monthly (about $70 to $90); his pay was supplemented by an additional 700 rubles per month from the Soviet Red Cross. According to Oswald's diary, his total income was about equal to that of the director of the factory where he worked.

The Warren Commission, however, found no basis for associating Oswald's high income with Soviet intelligence activity. I disagree. Oswald admits in his diary that monies he received from the Soviet Red Cross were actually from a Soviet intelligence agency.

Was Oswald Trained as an Intelligence Operative?

While in Minsk, Oswald had a membership in a hunting club, which was of special interest to the Warren Commission. The CIA advised the Commission that hunting societies such as the one to which Oswald belonged were very popular in the Soviet Union and that memberships were frequently sponsored by factories for their employees. The CIA, in its report to the Commission, advised that "a Soviet *citizen* may join a Hunting Society…at his place of employment." Of note is the inference that membership applies to Soviet citizens and not to stateless foreigners, Oswald's status at the time. The CIA report concludes, "The foregoing regulations *are believed* to apply also to foreigners residing in the Soviet Union."[29]

Did the KBG cause the issuance of Oswald's hunting license to a stateless person who was not a citizen of the Soviet Union so that KGB agents could continue Oswald's spy tradecraft and weapons training? I believe the answer to this question could be yes.

How Are Covert Intelligence Agents Trained?

I have not discovered any documents to prove that Oswald received training from the KGB in the "intelligence tradecrafts" of a secret undercover agent. The KGB had to assume that Oswald, a defector, would be investigated by the FBI upon his return to America and that his movements would be closely watched by FBI agents. I do find, however, that Oswald's behavior after returning to the United States from the Soviet Union suggests that he received some agent training. In making this assessment, I draw upon my CIA experience.

CIA employees who were recruited for covert intelligence operations abroad were trained at the "Farm," a covert facility located in the United States. During my various CIA assignments, I interfaced with my many agency operatives who received their undercover training there.

Most CIA employees working outside the United States are given a pseudonym, or alias. I used my pseudonym while overseas when communicating, both in paper documents and in cables transmitted electronically, with CIA headquarters or other CIA stations and bases located abroad. My special passports were issued in my true name showing me as an official of the Department of the Army.

Operational agents also receive training in "dead drop" information exchanges, or contact instructions for secret meetings, and in the use of fictitious personal identification documents. CIA agents also receive weapons training. I received small arms training while working at the CIA. Also, I was trained on how to conduct a discrete surveillance on persons of interest and how to detect someone conducting surveillance on me.

Most importantly, covert agents of the CIA and agents of other U.S. intelligence agencies operating in a foreign nation are taught discreet methods to follow when meeting with their handlers. It is always assumed that either the covert agent or his or her handler is under surveillance by counterintelligence agencies of the host government. The handler normally carries a diplomatic passport and most probably is assigned to his or her embassy or a diplomatic consulate. Thus, if caught by the host country the handler is afforded diplomatic immunity.

In the 1950s and early 1960s, if a CIA handler and covert agent needed to meet in person, this communication was normally accomplished by a brief coded written note sent to the covert agent using an alias and local post office box. The coded note would give a date, time, and place for another note exchange at a busy public venue, such as a supermarket.

En route to the designated meeting place, both the covert agent and handler would employ anti-surveillance practices. If either the covert agent or handler detected surveillance, the planned meeting would be aborted. If none was detected, the two would pass each other in opposite directions, and the covert agent would extend a greeting such as, "It's a surprise to see you here." The handler would extend an arm for a handshake and a small folded note would be passed to the covert agent's extended palm. After a few meaningless verbal exchanges, the two would continue with their decoy purpose for being in the meeting place.

Once outside the initial meeting venue, the covert agent would read the instruction note for a second meeting location, which would usually take place later that day or the next day. This second meeting, for example, could be on a park bench, at a restaurant, or during a large sporting event such as a bullfight. Hotel rooms were sometimes used, but there was always the danger that the hotel room could be "bugged" to record conservations. While traveling to the second meeting location, again the covert agent and the handler would follow anti-surveillance procedures.

As an example, while deployed to Tokyo, Japan, I would on occasion receive an assignment as a courier to deliver a pouch of classified documents to a secret CIA agent assigned to a base, also in Japan. At that time, initial contact instructions were delivered via encoded secret electronic cable traffic from station to base. The destination point for passing the pouch from me to the agent was about midway between our assigned workplaces. Following accepted protocol, we met at the first designated meeting place. I extended an arm for a handshake to pass a small note identifying our second meeting location, a nearby hotel with a rather large restaurant.

Evidence of Oswald's Intelligence Tradecraft Training

Many of Oswald's actions, following his return to the United States from the Soviet Union are indicative of intelligence tradecraft activity. I conclude Oswald himself made the various pieces of counterfeit identification, and there is no reason to believe that he received assistance from any person in establishing his alias except possibly the Soviet KGB.

Oswald worked briefly at Jaggars-Chiles-Stovall Co., a graphic arts company, in Dallas, Texas. While he was hired as a photo print trainee making prints of advertising material, the company also had the technical ability to produce photographic identification cards. After Oswald's arrest following the Kennedy assassination, a search of his wallet revealed a counterfeit Selective Service card with the name "Alex James Hidell" and a photograph of Oswald.

Also found among Oswald's personal effects after his arrest was a rubber stamping kit employed to produce a spurious international certificate of vaccination. The arresting officers found another forged Selective Service card with a picture of Oswald and the name "Alek J. Hidell" in Oswald's billfold. On November 22nd and 23rd, Oswald refused to tell Dallas Police Captain Fritz why this card was in his possession or to answer any questions concerning the card. On Sunday morning, November 24th, Oswald denied that he knew A. J. Hidell. Captain Fritz produced the Selective Service card bearing the name "Alek J. Hidell." Oswald became angry and said, "Now, I've told you all I'm going to tell you about that card in my billfolds—you have the card yourself and you know as much about it as I do." (This discrepancy between the findings in the wallet and billfold was not pursued by the Warren Commission.)

In addition, Oswald is known to have opened three post office boxes during 1962 and 1963 using an alias. On October 9, 1962, the same day that he arrived in Dallas from Fort Worth, and before establishing a residence there, he opened box 2915 at the Dallas General Post Office. This box was closed on May 14, 1963, shortly after Oswald had moved to New Orleans. That portion of the post office box application listing the names of those persons other than the applicant entitled to receive mail at the box was discarded in accordance with postal regulations after the box was closed; hence, it is not known what names other than Oswald's were listed on that form. However, Oswald is known to have received the assassination rifle under the name of A. Hidell and his Smith & Wesson revolver under the name of A. J. Hidell at that box.

According to Warren Commission Exhibit 796,[30] on June 3, 1963, Oswald, using the alias "Alek James Hidell" and a counterfeit Selective Service System draft classification card in the same bogus name, opened post office box 30061 at the Lafayette Square Substation in New Orleans, Louisiana. Marina Oswald and A. J. Hidell were listed as additional persons entitled to receive mail at this box.

Oswald's 1963 application for post office box in New Orleans.

Immediately before leaving alone to travel to Mexico City in late September 1963, Oswald submitted a request to forward his mail to Ruth Paine's address (his friend in Irving, Texas), and the box in New Orleans was closed on September 26th. On November 1, 1963, Oswald opened post office box 6225 at the Dallas Post Office Terminal Annex.

During his interrogation after the Kennedy assassination, Oswald admitted to U. S. Postal Inspector Harry Holmes that he had rented post office box 2915, in Dallas, but denied that he had received a package in this box addressed to Hidell. He also denied that he had received the rifle through this box. Holmes reminded Oswald that A. J. Hidell was listed also on post office box 30061 in New Orleans, as one entitled to receive mail. Oswald replied, "I don't know anything about that."

When asked why he lived at his rooming house under the name O. H. Lee, Oswald responded that the landlady simply made a mistake, because he told her that his name was Lee, meaning his first name. An examination of the rooming house register revealed that Oswald actually signed the name O. H. Lee.

Oswald's use of a pseudonym and frequent residential and employment changes in New Orleans, Fort Worth, and Dallas suggest that he was attempting to disrupt any ongoing FBI surveillance of his activities.

Oswald's travel to Mexico City in November, 1963, by multiple bus transfer also indicates an effort to disrupt any FBI surveillance of his plans. Also his movements while in Mexico City, including attendance at a bullfight, suggest a possible meeting with a KGB handler.

Did Oswald use the identity "Alex James Hidell" to obtain post office boxes as a way to receive coded communications from his KGB handlers? Were Oswald's continuous movements from various locations in Louisiana and Texas a conscious effort to disrupt surveillance of his movements by the FBI? Again, my answer is yes to both questions.

Oswald's Marriage

While living in Minsk, Oswald met Marina Prusakova, and they were married on April 30, 1961. The Warren Commission noted that a foreigner living in the USSR could not marry without the permission of the Soviet government. The Commissioners wrote that it seemed unlikely that the Soviet authorities would have permitted Oswald to marry and take his wife with him to the United States if they were contemplating using him alone as an agent. According to the Commission, the fact that he had a Russian wife would be likely, in the Soviets view, to increase any surveillance by American security agencies. Also, having a secret agent's wife in the United States would constitute a continuing risk of disclosure.

The Commission concluded Marina Oswald's lack of English training and her complete ignorance of the United States and its customs made it unlikely that she was a member of an "agent team" sent to the United States on a difficult and dangerous foreign assignment.

My opinion is just the opposite. Having Marina accompanying

Oswald made it less likely for the FBI to conclude that Oswald was a Soviet undercover agent on a dangerous mission. I believe that Marina was aware of some of Oswald's covert activities, but probably not his role in a conspiracy to assassinate President Kennedy.

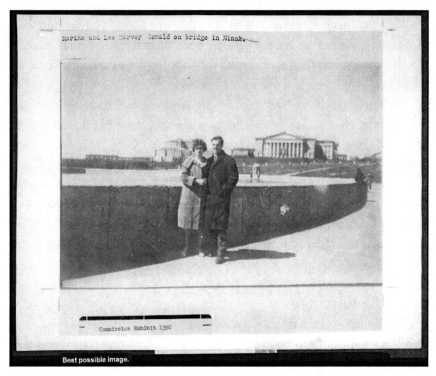

Oswald with his wife, Marina, in Minsk.

7 | Oswald Returns to the U.S.

In early February, 1961, prior to his marriage to Marina and following John F. Kennedy's election as U.S. President, Lee Harvey Oswald began making inquiries at the American Embassy in Moscow about renewing his passport and returning to the United States.[31] He was still officially an American citizen, had not applied for Russian citizenship, was living in Minsk with non-permanent papers available to foreigners, and could not leave Minsk without permission.

Oswald was seeking assurances that he would not be prosecuted for his defection to the Soviet Union. In an undated letter received by the American Embassy in Moscow, postmarked from Minsk on February 5, 1961, Oswald applied for reentry into the United States.

According to Warren Commission Exhibit 245, [32] the letter stated: "I desire to return to the United States, that is if we could come to some agreement concerning the dropping of any legal proceedings against me. If so, then I would be free to ask the Russian authorities to allow me to leave. If I could show them my American passport, I am of the opinion they would give me an exit…I cannot leave Minsk without permission, therefore I am writing rather than calling in person."

On February 28, 1961, an embassy official wrote Oswald that he would have to come to Moscow to discuss the passport and expatriation matters. After receiving the February letter, the Embassy official forwarded a dispatch to the U.S. Department of State in Washington, D.C., noting Oswald's letter and the reply. Embassy staff also inquired whether the department believed Oswald would be subject to prosecution on any grounds should he return to the United States and, if so, whether Oswald should be so informed. The embassy officials also sought the department's advice on whether there was any objection to returning Oswald's 1959 passport to him by mail, since that might facilitate his application for a Soviet exit visa.

On March 20, 1961, a second letter from Oswald, dated March 12, was received by the American Embassy. Oswald reiterates that he is unable to travel to Moscow without permission. He also points out that "there exist [sic] in the United States also a law in regards to resident foreigners from Socialist countries, traveling between cities."

While he writes that he understands that a personal interview would be preferred by embassy staff, he adds: "I do not think it would be appropriate for me to request to leave Minsk in order to visit the American Embassy. In any event, the granting of permission is a long drawn out affair, and I find that there is a hesitation on the part of local officials to even start the process."

When the embassy received Oswald's March letter, officials again consulted Washington. They proposed a response to Oswald repeating that he must come to Moscow if he wanted to discuss reentering the United States, and pointing out that the Soviet government did not object to such visits by American citizens. This letter was mailed to Oswald on March 24, 1961.

A Letter from Moscow

Two months later, another communication exchange occurred that, in my view, raises an interesting question. On May 26, 1961, Embassy officials sent a dispatch to the State Department advising that they had received another letter from Oswald the previous day, postmarked Moscow, May 16, 1961.[33] At this time, by all accounts Oswald was living in Minsk, approximately 450 miles from Moscow.

How did Oswald, who was living in Minsk, send a letter to the U. S. Embassy from Moscow, or who sent it for him?

In this May letter, Oswald said he wanted "to make it clear" that he was asking for full guarantees that he would not be prosecuted "under any circumstances" should he return to the United States. Oswald went on to say that if the embassy could not give him these assurances, he would "endeavor to use my relatives in the United States, to see about getting something done in Washington." He also informed the embassy that he was married to a Russian woman who would want to accompany him back to his native country, and he once again repeated his reluctance to come to Moscow.

On July 11, 1961, The State Department sent a reply to the American Embassy stating that it was not entirely clear what the description "without citizenship" meant: "Whether he is without Soviet citizenship or without any citizenship." In the absence of any evidence showing that Oswald had lost his United States citizenship, the department concluded that he apparently maintains that technical status. The reply continued: "Whether he is entitled to the protection of the United States pending any further developments concerning his precise status is a matter which will be left to the embassy's discretion in the event an emergency situation should arise."

On Saturday, July 8, 1961, however, before the embassy had received that response from Washington, Oswald appeared without warning at the American Embassy in Moscow. Oswald called an embassy officer on the house phone and, after a brief talk, the officer asked Oswald to return the next Monday. After the visit, Oswald telephoned his wife and told her to come to Moscow, which she did the next day. Oswald returned alone to the American Embassy on Monday, where the officer questioned him about his life in Russia.

How did Oswald, a stateless person living in Minsk, arrive in Moscow since he still needed the approval of the Soviet government to travel within the USSR?

During the interview with the embassy officer, Oswald filled out an application to renew his American passport since Oswald's existing passport was set to expire on September 10, 1961. Both Oswald and the officer agreed that it was extremely unlikely that he would be able to obtain the requisite Soviet departure documents before that time.

On June 1, 1962, immediately following U.S. State Department approval for Oswald and his wife, Marina, to enter the United States, they left Moscow by train destined for Rotterdam, Netherlands. On June 4th they boarded the *SS Maasdam* at Rotterdam and arrived in

New York on June 13th. After a brief sightseeing tour of New York City, Oswald and Marina traveled to Fort Worth, Texas.

An Analysis of Oswald's Time in the USSR

My review of the relevant facts of Oswald's travel to the Soviet Union from New Orleans, Louisiana, on September 17, 1959, and ending with his departure from Moscow on June 1, 1962, supports the following opinions: *During his travel to the Soviet Union, his work and residence while there, and his departure, Oswald received special treatment, including money, from the Soviet government's intelligence agencies. Also, while in Minsk, Oswald was trained to be a secret agent of the Soviet Union.*

Numerous facts, documented by the Warren Commission, support my hypotheses.

Travel to the Soviet Union. Oswald applied for his passport two days following his release from Marine Corps active duty with the intention of traveling by ship, air, and train from New Orleans, Louisiana, to Moscow without discussing his travel plans with family or friends. He claimed to have saved $1,500 for travel expenses while in the Marines from his monthly pay as a private. Arriving in Helsinki, he received from the Soviet Consulate a visa to travel to Moscow in two days rather than the five or six days needed for other travelers to the Soviet Union. At the Moscow train station on October 16, 1959, Oswald was met by KBG Intourist guides who arranged and paid for his lodging in Moscow while he was being processed for a stateless foreign visitor identification document and travel to Minsk.

Employment in Minsk. Oswald arrived in Minsk on January 7, 1960, and was placed in a radio TV factory job earning a higher-than-average monthly salary paid to the average factory worker. That salary was supplemented by the KGB so that his monthly income was equal to the factory director's salary.

Residence in Minsk. Oswald's apartment in Minsk was upscale and better than most other apartments in that city. According to Oswald, since his monthly rent was mostly paid by the Soviet government, he paid almost nothing.

Francis Gary Powers Trial. While living in Minsk, Oswald wrote to his brother, Robert, that he saw Francis Gary Powers in Moscow. This sighting could have occurred only during the Powers interrogation prior to his trial or at the actual trial in August 1960. Soviet Union government approval for Oswald's travel to Moscow was required, as admitted by Oswald in a letter to the American Embassy in Moscow. Most certainly, this travel approval and funding was underwritten by the KGB.

Hunting Club Membership. Oswald was classified as a stateless person while residing in the Soviet Union. Still, Oswald obtained a hunting club membership while in Minsk. According to Soviet government policy, Soviet citizenship was required for obtaining a hunting club membership. Oswald was not a citizen of the Soviet Union. Thus, to receive a hunting club membership required the approval of the Soviet government.

Communication with the American Embassy in Moscow. While purportedly living in Minsk, the U.S. Embassy in Moscow received a letter from him postmarked from Moscow. Then, on July 8, 1961, Oswald suddenly appeared without warning at the Embassy. By Oswald's own admission, his travel from Minsk required prior Soviet government approval.

Travel from the Soviet Union. Soviet government approval was needed for Oswald to exit the Soviet Union. He was able to receive these approvals and the documents required to leave the country in an extremely fast time starting from the return of his U.S. passport by the American Embassy.

Chapter 8 reviews several of Oswald's suspicious activities, after arriving in the United States, to further support my thesis that the Soviet Union was involved in the assassination of President John F. Kennedy.

8

Oswald's Activities in the U.S.

The Warren Commission report goes into considerable detail tracing Oswald's employment, places of residence, and travels in and around two cities in Texas, Fort Worth and Dallas, and New Orleans, Louisiana, after his return from the Soviet Union. The chronology is based on several interviews by the FBI with both Lee Harvey Oswald and his wife, Marina.[34]

Oswald's Residences and Employment

Oswald and his family arrived in New York City on June 13, 1962, and traveled to Fort Worth, Texas, where they lived temporarily with Oswald's brother, Robert. Sometime in July or August 1962, Oswald rented an apartment on Mercedes Street in Fort Worth where he and Marina lived briefly.

Oswald obtained a job in July of 1962 as a sheet metal worker with a company in Fort Worth. His performance for that company was satisfactory. Even though he told Marina that he had been fired, he left voluntarily on October 8, 1962, and the couple moved to Dallas. On October 9, 1962, he went to the Dallas office of the Texas Employment Commission where he expressed a reluctance to work in the industrial field and began looking for other types of work.

On October 11, 1962, the Employment Commission referred Oswald to a commercial advertising photography firm in Dallas where he was employed as a trainee starting October 12th. Even though

Oswald indicated that he liked photographic work, his employer found that he was not an efficient worker and had difficulty in working with other employees. Oswald was discharged on April 6, 1963. Meanwhile, on March 3, 1963, the Oswalds moved out of their Dallas Elsbeth Street apartment to an upstairs apartment several blocks away at 214 West Neely Street.

When Oswald left Dallas for New Orleans on April 24, 1963, he left his wife and child at the home of a friend, Mrs. Ruth Paine, of Irving, Texas. After securing a job and an apartment there, Oswald asked his wife to join him. Mrs. Paine drove Oswald's family to New Orleans.

In New Orleans he obtained work as a greaser and oiler of coffee processing machines for the William B. Reily Co., beginning on May 10, 1963. He lost his job on July 19, 1963, because his work was not satisfactory and because he spent too much time loitering in the garage next door, where he read rifle and hunting magazines.

While in New Orleans, Oswald planned a trip to Mexico. Following his return to Dallas from this sojourn in September, Oswald obtained a job at the Texas Book Depository Company, and began working there on October 16, 1963.

Oswald's Use of Post Office Mail Boxes

Oswald is known to have opened three post office boxes during 1962 and 1963. On October 9, 1962, the same day that he arrived in Dallas from Fort Worth and before establishing a residence there, he opened box 2915 at the Dallas General Post Office. This box was closed on May 14, 1963, shortly after Oswald had moved to New Orleans. Oswald is known to have received the assassination rifle under the name of A. Hidell and his Smith & Wesson revolver under the name of A. J. Hidell at box 2915.

On June 3, 1963, Oswald opened box 30061 at the Lafayette Square Substation in New Orleans. Marina Oswald and A. J. Hidell were listed as additional persons entitled to receive mail at this box. Immediately before leaving for Mexico City in late September, Oswald submitted a request to forward his mail to Ruth Paine, who now lived in Irving, Texas, and the box was closed on September 26th.

On November 1, 1963, he opened box 6225 at the Dallas Post Office Terminal Annex. The Fair Play for Cuba Committee and the American Civil Liberties Union were listed as also being entitled to receive mail at this box.

Oswald's Attempt to Assassinate General Walker

On April 10, 1963, Oswald attempted to assassinate Major General Edwin Walker, an active and controversial figure on the American political scene after he resigned from the U.S. Army in 1961. Previously, during the weekend of March 9th and 10th, Oswald photographed the alley behind General Walker's home. At about the same time, Oswald photographed the rear of the Walker home and a nearby railroad track and right-of-way. He prepared and studied a notebook in which he outlined a plan to shoot General Walker, and he looked at bus schedules. He went to the Walker residence on the evening of April 6th or 7th, planning to make his attack. However, he changed his plans and hid his rifle nearby. He decided to act on the following Wednesday, April 10th, when a neighborhood church was planning a meeting. Oswald reasoned that the gathering would create a diversion and help him escape.

On Wednesday, Oswald left a note for Marina telling her what to do if he was apprehended. He retrieved his rifle and fired at General Walker, and the bullet narrowly missed Walker's head. Oswald secreted his rifle again and took the bus home.

The note, a Russian volume titled *"Book of Useful Advice,"* is most interesting. According to the Warren Commission Exhibit 1,[35] Oswald, in Russian, left eleven instructions for Marina, including "This is the key to the mailbox which is located in the main post office in the city on Ervay Street. This is same street where the drugstore, in which you always waited in which is located."

Item number two instructs Marina to "…send information as to what has happened to me to the Embassy and include newspaper clippings…I believe that the Embassy will come quickly to your assistance on learning everything." I assume Oswald is referring to the Soviet Embassy in Washington, D.C.

When Oswald told Marina that he had attempted to assassinate

General Walker, she became angry and made him promise never to repeat such an act. She testified that she had no advance knowledge of Oswald's plans and that she kept his letter intending to give it to the authorities "if something like that should be repeated again."[36] He told Marina that he was sorry he had missed General Walker.

The Warren Commission opined that Oswald did not lack the determination and other traits required to carry out a carefully planned killing of another human being and was willing to consummate such a purpose if he thought there was sufficient reason to do so.

Was Oswald's assassination attempt on General Walker a practice run prior to any attempt to kill President Kennedy? Did Oswald prepare the note of instructions on November 21st, the night he stayed at the Paine residence prior to President Kennedy's assassination on November 22nd?"

Dallas Press Reporting on Kennedy Visit

The public in the State of Texas first became aware of President Kennedy's proposed visit to Texas on September 13, 1963, when the planning was reported in the media. The Warren Commission determined that the President's intended visit to Texas in the fall of 1963 aroused interest throughout the state. Dallas newspapers provided readers with a steady stream of information and speculation about the trip. On September 13th, a front-page article in the *Dallas Times Herald* announced that President Kennedy was planning a brief one-day tour of four Texas cities—Dallas, Fort Worth, San Antonio, and Houston. The Dallas papers cited White House sources on September 26th as confirming the President's intention to visit Texas on November 21nd and 22nd, with Dallas scheduled as one of the stops.

Articles, editorials, and letters to the editor in the *Dallas Morning News* and the *Dallas Times Herald* after September 13th reported on the feeling in the community toward the forthcoming Presidential visit. Although some were critical, the news stories reflected the desire of Dallas officials to welcome the President with dignity and courtesy. An editorial in the Times-Herald of September 17th called on the people of Dallas to be "congenial hosts" even though "Dallas didn't vote for Mr. Kennedy in 1960, may not endorse him in '64." On October 3rd the Dallas Morning News quoted U.S. Representative Joe Pool's hope

Dallas Times Herald newspaper article dated September 16, 1963.

that President Kennedy would receive a "good welcome" and would not face demonstrations like those encountered by Vice President Lyndon Johnson during the 1960 presidential campaign.[37]

Oswald's Visit to Mexico City

Oswald applied for a tourist card to visit Mexico at the Mexican Consulate in New Orleans where he was living on September 19, 1963, six days after the White House announced President Kennedy's planned visit to Dallas.

Oswald's trip to Mexico City in late September and early October 1963, less than two months before he assassinated President Kennedy, has provoked speculation that it was related in some way to a conspiracy to murder the President. Rumors include assertions that he made a clandestine flight from Mexico to Cuba and back and that he received a large sum of money, estimated to be $5,000, which he brought back to Dallas.

The Warren Commission, however, found no credible evidence that Oswald went to Mexico to pursue a plan to assassinate President Kennedy, received any instructions related to such an action while there, or received large sums of money from any Mexican source.

Marina Oswald testimony before the Warren Commission was that Oswald told her that the purpose of the trip was to evade the American prohibition on travel to Cuba and to reach that country, although she denied that she knew of the trip until she testified.[38] Oswald cautioned her that the trip and its purpose were to be kept strictly secret. She also testified that he had planned to reach Cuba earlier by hijacking an airliner flying out of New Orleans. She refused to cooperate and urged him to give that plan up, which he finally did. Witnesses who spoke with Oswald while he was on a bus going to Mexico City also testified that Oswald told them he intended to reach Cuba and that he hoped to meet Fidel Castro.[39]

The Warren Commission investigated several allegations of conspiratorial contact between Oswald and agents of the Cuban government. One allegation posited that Oswald had made a previous trip to Mexico City. According to a Cuban expatriate publication, Fidel Castro, in a speech he delivered five days after the assassination while

OSWALD'S MEXICAN TOURIST CARD AND APPLICATION

APPLICATION FOR
TOURIST CARD

(COMMISSION EXHIBIT 2481)

TOURIST CARD ▶

(COMMISSION EXHIBIT 2478)

Best possible image.

Oswald's Mexican tourist card application

he was under the influence of liquor, said: "The first time Oswald was in Cuba," implying that Oswald had made one or more surreptitious trips to Cuba.

The Warren Commission Exhibit 2763[40] is a memorandum from FBI Director Hoover to the State Department with copies to the CIA director and the chief of the Secret Service. It notes that the FBI was in receipt of two letters postmarked at Havana, Cuba, implicating Oswald in a conspiracy to assassinate President Kennedy. One letter, dated November 10, 1963, was addressed to Oswald in care of the mail office, Dallas, Texas. The second letter, dated November 28, 1963, was addressed to Robert Kennedy, Secretary of Justice [sic], Washington, D.C.

When Oswald spoke to the Cuban and Soviet consular officials in Mexico City, he said that he intended to travel to the Soviet Union and requested a visa to visit to Cuba while en route to the Soviet Union. In support of his application, Oswald presented three documents: his U.S. passport, which noted that he had lived in the USSR for three years; his USSR labor card written in Russian; and his own letters written in the Russian. He also presented evidence that he was married to a Russian woman.

The Cubans would not, however, give him a visa until he had received one from the Soviets, which involved a delay of several months. The Cuban Embassy employee, complying with her duties, took down all of the information, completed the appropriate application, and informally telephoned the Soviet consulate with the intention of doing what she could to facilitate issuance of a Russian visa to Lee Harvey Oswald. Officials at the Soviet consulate told her that there would be a delay of about four months in processing the case. This answer annoyed Oswald since, according to his statement, he was in a great hurry to obtain visas that would enable him to travel to the USSR. Oswald insisted on his right to do so in view of his background, his loyalty, and his activities on behalf of the Cuban movement. The Cuban Embassy stated that when Oswald understood that it was not possible to give him a visa, he became very excited or angry.

The Warren Commission's report included significant findings about a final letter written by Oswald to the Soviet Embassy in Washington, D.C. following his return from Mexico in October 1963. Oswald's letter to the Soviet Embassy, dated November 9, 1963, began by stating that it was written "to inform you of recent events since my meetings with Comrade Kostin in the Embassy of the Soviet Union, Mexico City, Mexico." The envelope bears a postmark which appears to be November 12, 1963. Ruth Paine, Oswald's friend in Irving, Texas, testified before the Warren Commission that Oswald spent a weekend at her home working on the letter and that she observed a preliminary draft.[41] A paper, which was identified as one of these drafts, was found among Oswald's effects after the Kennedy assassination. According to Marina Oswald, her husband retyped the envelope ten times.

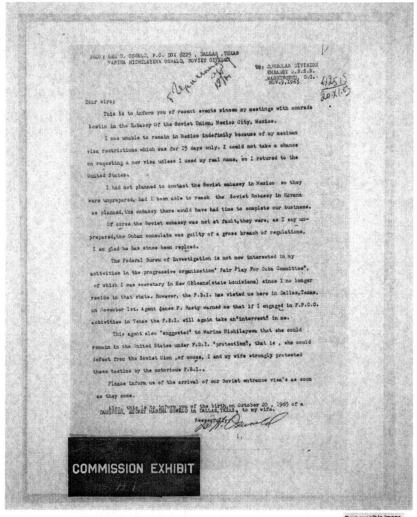

Best possible image.

Oswald's letter to the Soviet Embassy in Washington, D.C., following his return from Mexico in 1963.

Information produced for the Warren Commission by the CIA concludes that the person referred to in the letter as "Comrade Kostin" was probably Valeriy Vladimirovich Kostikov, a member of the consular staff of the Soviet Union in Mexico City. He is also one of the KGB officers stationed at that embassy. It was standard Soviet procedure for KGB officers stationed in embassies and in consulates to carry on the

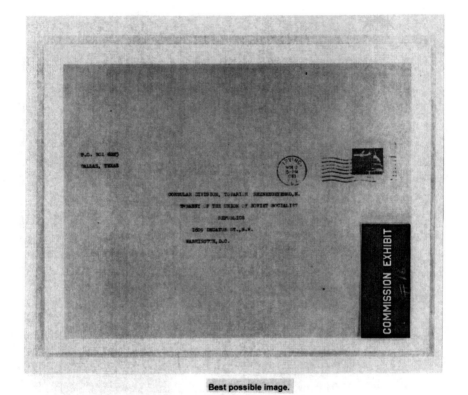

Best possible image.

normal duties of such a position in addition to undercover activities.[42]

The CIA advised the Warren Commission that the Cuban consul responded by noting that the employee referred to in Oswald's letter was Senor Eusebio Azque (also "Ascue"), the man with whom Oswald argued at the Cuban Embassy, who left Mexico for Cuba on permanent transfer on November, 18, 1963, four days before the Kennedy assassination. Azque had been in Mexico for eighteen years and, wrote the CIA, "we speculate that Silvia Duran or some Soviet official might have mentioned [his transfer] if Oswald complained about Azque's altercation with him."

When asked by the Warren Commission to explain the letter to the Soviet Embassy in Washington, D.C., Marina Oswald was unable to add anything to an understanding of its contents. However, when the draft and the final document are studied, especially when crossed-out words are taken into account, it becomes apparent that Oswald was intentionally clouding his true reasons to make his trip to Mexico sound mysterious and important.

For example, the first sentence in the second paragraph of the letter reads, "I was unable to remain in Mexico indefinitely because of my Mexican visa restrictions which was for 15 days only." The Commission determined Oswald's tourist card was still valid for a full week when he left Mexico on October 3rd.

The letter also reads, "I could not take a chance on requesting a new visa unless I used my real name, so I returned to the United States." In fact, he did use his real name for his tourist card and in dealings with the Cuban Embassy, the Russian Embassy, and elsewhere. Oswald did use the name, Lee, on the trip, but he did so only sporadically and probably as the result of a clerical error.

Ultimately, based upon its knowledge of Oswald, the Commission concluded that the letter constitutes no more than a clumsy effort to ingratiate himself with the Soviet Embassy.

I postulate other conclusions about Oswald's letter to the Soviet Embassy. I believe the letter was a coded communication reporting on his travel to Mexico City. Also, Oswald is reporting that he had not followed his KGB training regarding his travel to Mexico City…borrowing an expression used by some of my former CIA associates, "He screwed-up and was covering his ass."

I believe Oswald was covering up his mistakes in his reporting to the KGB handlers at the Soviet Embassy in Washington, D.C.

An Alternate View of Oswald's Trip to Mexico

I found the Warren Commission's investigation into Oswald's travel to Mexico City from September 26, 1963, to October 3, 1963, to be disjointed, difficult to follow logically, and inconsistent with established investigative practice. I conclude that the investigative finding is very germane to one of the Commission's possible motives for Oswald's assassination of President Kennedy: Oswald's avowed commitment to Marxism and Communism and his defection to the Soviet Union.

Consider this sentence in the Commission's report: "Oswald contacted the Russian and Cuba Embassies again during his stay in Mexico. He had no greater success than he had before." The use of the words "again" and "before" infers that Oswald had previously traveled to Mexico. This assertion would appear to confirm Fidel Castro's statement in a speech he delivered five days after the assassination, when he said, "The first time Oswald was in Cuba," also implying that Oswald had made one or more surreptitious trips to Cuba prior to the October visit to Mexico.

Marina testified before the Commission that when Oswald returned to Texas he was convinced that his trip had been a failure and was disappointed that he was unable to go to Cuba. A month later, in the painstakingly composed letter to the Soviet Embassy in Washington, Oswald ascribed his failure to "a gross breach of regulations" on the part of the Cuban Embassy. "Of course," he wrote, "the Soviet Embassy was not at fault, they were, as I say unprepared."

Ultimately, then, the Commission reported that its investigation produced no evidence that Oswald's trip to Mexico was in any way connected with the assassination of President Kennedy, and that it uncovered no evidence that the Cuban government had any involvement in the assassination.

Also, the Commission reported it had been advised by the CIA and FBI that secret and reliable sources corroborated the statements of Cuban Embassy employee, Senora Duran, and that the Cuban government had no relationship with Lee Harvey Oswald other than that described by Senora Duran. Then-Secretary of State Rusk also testified that after the assassination "there was very considerable concern in Cuba as to whether they would be held responsible and what the effect of that might be on their own position and their own safety."

I accept the Commission's conclusion that Cuba was not involved directly with Kennedy assassination; however, I conclude that Cuba could have been either an unwitting or active participant in Oswald's escape plan following the assassination. I believe that Oswald planned to fly to Cuba and then connect to a flight to Moscow. To facilitate that plan, Oswald traveled to Mexico City four weeks before the Kennedy assassination and visited both the Cuban and Soviet Union embassies in an effort to obtain permission to enter Cuba and the Soviet Union. But, consider these questions:

Why did Oswald travel to Mexico City immediately after the Texas press reported on President Kennedy's visit to Dallas? Was Oswald planning to escape to Cuba and then to the Soviet Union after he assassinated President Kennedy?

If the answers to these two questions is yes, as I believe, a third question must be raised:

Is it possible that the Soviet Union may have been involved in the assassination of President John F. Kennedy on November 22, 1963?

9

Motives for Killing President Kennedy

Many individuals and researchers have speculated about Lee Harvey Oswald's motives for assassinating President John F. Kennedy. One view is that Oswald was in some way associated with or used by agencies of the U.S. government, specifically the FBI and the CIA.

Oswald was investigated by the FBI after his return to the United States from the Soviet Union in June 1962. Those who support the view that Oswald had a working relationship with the FBI base their conclusion on an entry in Oswald's "Historical Diary," giving the name and telephone number of an agent from the FBI office in Dallas. Others believe that Oswald was a CIA agent or had some relationship with the CIA, and that this association explained the supposed ease with which he received passports and visas during his trips into and out of the USSR.

The directors of the CIA and the FBI at the time, Allan Dulles and J. Edgar Hoover, testified before the Warren Commission that Oswald was never employed by their agencies in any capacity. Based on this testimony and its own investigation of federal files, the Commission concluded that Oswald was not and had never been an agent of any U.S. government entity and that no U.S. government agency was involved in planning for or actually killing President Kennedy. In my research, I found no facts to contradict the Commission's conclusion.

The Commission's Search for Oswald's Motive

Finding no evidence in the circumstances immediately surrounding the assassination that any person other than Lee Harvey Oswald was involved in the killing of the President, the Warren Commission directed an intensive investigation into his life for the purpose, among others, of detecting any possible traces that at some point he became involved in a conspiracy culminating in the assassination of President Kennedy.

The Commission did not make any definitive determination of Oswald's motives. However, its report did endeavor to isolate factors in Oswald's character that might have influenced his decision to assassinate President Kennedy: his deep-rooted resentment of all authority, which was expressed in hostility toward every society in which he lived; his inability to enter into meaningful relationships with people and a continuous pattern of rejecting his environment in favor of new surroundings; his urge to try to find a place in history and despair at times over failures in his various undertakings; and his capacity for violence as evidenced by his attempt to kill Major General Walker (see Chapter 8).[43]

But to arrive at a conclusive motive for killing President Kennedy, the Commission looked into a fifth possibility: Oswald's avowed commitment to Marxism and Communism, and his understanding and interpretation of their tenets. As he embraced these philosophies, he became antagonistic toward the United States, defected to the Soviet Union, was unable to reconcile with life in the United States even after his disenchantment with the Soviet Union, and failed in his attempt to go to Cuba.

Oswald's Connection to the Soviet Union

To evaluate rumors and speculations that Oswald may have been an agent of the Soviet Union, the Warren Commission investigated the facts surrounding Oswald's stay there from 1959 to 1962. The Commission stated it was thus fulfilling its obligation to probe all facts of possible relevance to the assassination, and did not suggest by this investigation that the rulers of the Soviet Union believed that their political interests would be advanced by the assassination of President Kennedy.[44]

On the question of the Soviet Union's involvement in the assassination, then-Secretary of State Dean Rusk testified before the Commission on June 10, 1964, that he had not seen any evidence that would indicate that the Soviet Union had an interest in or was involved in the removal of President Kennedy. "Although there had been grave differences between Chairman Khrushchev and President Kennedy, I think there were evidences of a certain mutual respect that had developed over some of the experiences, both good and bad, through which these two men had lived." He went on to say he believed "Both of them were aware that any Chairman of the Soviet Union and any President of the United States bear special responsibility for the general peace of the world. Indeed without exaggeration, one could almost say the existence of the northern hemisphere in this nuclear age."[45]

The Commission accepted Secretary Rusk's estimate as reasonable and objective but recognized that a precise assessment of Soviet intentions or interests was most difficult.[46] Thus, the Commission concluded, "There was no evidence to show that Oswald was employed, persuaded, or encouraged by any foreign government to assassinate President Kennedy or that he was an agent of any foreign government."[47]

As my research shows, however, there were numerous clues in Oswald's movements, actions, and writings that point to another conclusion: *Lee Harvey Oswald was an agent of the KGB and, as such, was used by the Soviet Union to assassinate President Kennedy.*

Soviet Motives for Killing President Kennedy

In re-examining the events that unfolded as President Kennedy took office, a number of factors could have motivated Nikita Khrushchev to pursue a KGB assassination plan. For example, on August 3, 1960, Soviet Ambassador to the United States Andrei Gromyko sent a report to "Comrade N.S. Khrushchev" assessing presidential candidate Kennedy's position on U.S.-Soviet Union policy issues.[48] Gromyko pointed out the provocative flights of American U-2 airplanes from 1956 to 1960, which disrupted an imminent summit conference between President Eisenhower and Khrushchev. He also noted that even though Kennedy had announced publicly that he would not have authorized such flights, Kennedy would not hesitate to use the shooting down by the Soviets of the U-2 plane piloted by Gary Powers to his political advantage.

Ambassador Gromyko concluded that Kennedy's view of the balance of power was the main reason for the United States to avoid engaging in summit talks with the Soviet Union. He quoted Kennedy as saying, "Above all, we must make sure that henceforward we conduct talks from a position of strength—of military strength, economic strength, strength of ideas, and strength of purpose."[49]

In addition to Gromyko's assessment, I believe five incidents stand out as cogent reasons that could have motivated Khrushchev to pursue a KGB plan to assassinate President Kennedy.

Kennedy's Inaugural Address. On January 20, 1961, I proudly watched President Kennedy's motorcade pass on Pennsylvania Avenue en route to the White House following his Inaugural Address. I had just heard his impressive concluding remarks: "In the long history of the world, only a few generations have been granted the role of defending freedom in its hour of maximum danger. I do not shrink from this responsibility—I welcome it. I do not believe that any of us would exchange places with any other people or any other generation. The energy, the faith, the devotion which we bring to this endeavor will light our country and all who serve—and the glow from that fire can truly light the world."[50]

I believe these stirring remarks, which were an inspiration to all Americans, were viewed as threatening to the Soviets. Kennedy's policies and actions as President reinforced this conclusion.

America's Missile Program. The results of Kennedy's forward-thinking rhetoric lead to his decision to accelerate America's missile program. President Kennedy understood the need to restore America's confidence and intended not merely to match the Soviets, but to surpass them. On May 25, 1961, President Kennedy asked the U.S. Congress for an additional $7 billion to $9 billion over the next five years to underwrite a space exploration program that would surpass similar efforts by the Soviets.

Bay of Pigs Invasion. In another bold move, President Kennedy approved the invasion of the Bay of Pigs in Cuba. The CIA-sponsored invasion began on April 15, 1961, with bombing raids by B-26 liberators intending to destroy the Cuban Air Force to be followed by a ground assault two days later. Even though the invasion failed, Premier Khrushchev continued to be concerned that President Kennedy would attempt another military action against Communist Cuba.

Cuban Missile Crisis. Perhaps the most important reason for Khrushchev to consider killing President Kennedy was the U.S. Navy's blockade of Soviet shipments to Cuba and Kennedy's demand that Russian missiles be removed from the island. The "Cuban Missile Crisis" was a serious military confrontation between the Soviet Union and the United States that could have resulted in World War III.

In mid-October 1962, an American U-2 spy plane secretly photographed nuclear missile sites being built by the Soviet Union in Cuba. The sites were for medium- and intermediate-range nuclear missiles with the ability to strike the southeastern United States. The President met in secret with his advisors for thirteen days reviewing a very precarious situation, which could potentially endanger the lives of millions of Americans.

At the end of these deliberations, President Kennedy demanded that the Soviet government remove its missiles and atomic warheads from Cuba. He imposed a naval blockade or "quarantine," as he called it, of Cuba to prevent passage of Soviet supply ships to its ports. Ultimately, Khrushchev and the Soviet Union chose not to attack the blockade, avoiding the risk of war, and agreed to remove its missiles from Cuba.

American citizens and government officials alike were unsure how Khrushchev would respond as the Soviets ships approached the naval blockade. During this emergency, a select cadre of the CIA Office of Security's physical security staff was included in the agency's wartime emergency plan to relocate its headquarters to a site outside of the Washington D.C. metro area. If the President declared a national emergency, I was one of the security officers required to go to the relocation site armed with a Smith and Wesson .38 caliber pistol and an ample supply of bullets. During the thirteen days of the missile crisis, I had a packed suitcase ready for my deployment to the CIA relocation site.

Potential Assassination of Castro. As a result of President Kennedy's scrutiny of events in Cuba, Khrushchev had reason to be concerned that the President would authorize the CIA to assassinate Cuban President Fidel Castro, enabling CIA-sponsored pro-freedom Cuban operatives to regain control of Cuba. Any real or perceived threats against Cuba, a firm Communist ally in the Americas, no doubt incited Khrushchev's ire.

Oswald's Hasty Return to America

The Cuban missile crisis most certainly humiliated Khrushchev. His submission to President Kennedy's demand that Russian missiles be removed from Cuba, as seen by the world, clearly demonstrated the United States superiority. Thus, I believe sometime in late January or early February, 1961, Lee Harvey Oswald received his marching orders from the KGB: "Return to the United States." Oswald, after spending sixteen months inside the Soviet Union, had most certainly completed the intelligence training necessary for any assignment (see Chapter 6).

As detailed in Chapter 7, Oswald's letters attempting to return to the United States raise numerous questions on how he actually accomplished the movements that lead to his departure. In February 1961, the American Embassy in Moscow received a letter from Oswald postmarked from Minsk, USSR, asking to be readmitted to the United States. This was the first time that the Embassy had heard from or about Oswald since November 1959. The Embassy responded by inviting Oswald to come to Moscow to discuss the matter. Oswald at first protested because of the difficulty of obtaining Soviet permission. He wrote two more protesting letters during the following four months, but received no indication that the embassy would allow him to handle the matter by mail.

While the U.S. Department of State was clarifying its position on this matter, Oswald unexpectedly appeared in Moscow in July 1961. A few days later, Marina Oswald flew to Moscow, and both were interviewed by officials in the American Embassy.

The Warren Commission asked the Department of State and the CIA to comment on whether Oswald's travel to Moscow without permission signified special treatment by the Soviet Union. From their responses, it appears that since Marina Oswald possessed a Soviet citizen's internal passport, she did not require prior approval to make the trip. However, the CIA advised the Commission, bearers of a Soviet "passport for foreigners" are required to obtain travel authorization… if they desire to leave the city where they are domiciled. This same requirement is believed to apply to persons, such as Oswald, holding a Soviet stateless passport.

The Warren Commission also asked the State Department to comment on the movement of U.S. citizens in the Soviet Union. The department reaffirmed that "clergy, correspondents, and students with U.S. passports must obtain permission from Soviet authorities before taking any trips. U.S. technical advisers must notify officials of their project before they travel, and these officials personally inform the militia."

As a result of this knowledge, State Department officials testified that if Oswald went to Moscow without permission, and this fact was known to the Soviet authorities, he would have been fined or reprimanded. Oswald was not, of course, an average foreign resident. He was a defector from a foreign country and the bearer of a Soviet internal stateless passport. The Soviet authorities probably knew about Oswald's trip even if he did not obtain advance permission, since in most instances the Soviet militia guards at the American Embassy would ask for the documents of unidentified persons entering the embassy grounds.

These statements to the Warren Commission by State Department and CIA officials lead me to conclude the Soviet government was aware of Lee Harvey and Marina Oswald's travel plans prior to their departure from Minsk to Moscow in July 1961.

A Concluding Observation

My final observation about the assassination of President Kennedy is that the Warren Commission in its investigation of the killing of Kennedy deliberately avoided a comprehensive examination of certain facts that could have supported the uncovering of a foreign conspiracy. This intentional oversight, in my view, avoided a possible U.S. nuclear war with the Soviet Union during a very tense period in relations between the two countries, which had been exacerbated by the 1962 Cuban Missile Crisis.

If indeed this hypnosis is correct, then the Warren Commission published the correct conclusion when it reported there is "no evidence to show that Oswald was employed, persuaded, or encouraged by any foreign government to assassinate President Kennedy or that he was an agent of any foreign government."

Contrary to the Commission's findings, however, I now believe it is conceivable and plausible to conclude that Oswald could have been a secret agent of the Soviet KGB intelligence service at the time of the assassination. I believe the facts presented in the chapters of this book as well as the questions raised by Oswald's actions and letters lead a reasonable person to conclude that the Union of Soviet Socialist Republics could have been involved in a conspiracy to assassinate President Kennedy and that the KGB recruited Lee Harvey Oswald to carry out that task.

Postscript

In addition to the primary and secondary documents reviewed for this treatise, I have based the theories presented in this book on my experiences as an employee of the Central Intelligence Agency (CIA). I also used my direct experience with former Soviet intelligence officers after the break-up of the Soviet Union to support my belief that the Soviet KGB was active in Japan during the 1950s.

Training Former Soviet Intelligence Officers in Bank Security

Shortly after the Soviet Union broke apart in December 1991, I was contacted by an executive at an American company headquartered in northern New Jersey. I was told that I had been identified as America's foremost bank security expert and that his company wished to engage me to instruct former Soviet intelligence officers who were working at or seeking employment in the banks that had emerged in the new Russia.

I delayed for a week before responding; I was in a dilemma. On the one hand, it would be contrary to my principles to work with Russian intelligence, either directly or indirectly, even through a secondary source. This view was especially cogent in light of my opinions as expressed in this book.

On the other hand, however, I believed that if the new Russian government was to survive as capitalist nation, it would be imperative for the newly formed banks to have security procedures and protocols in place. These safeguards were necessary, I believed, to protect against potential criminal activity and ensure that Russian citizens and businesses would safely invest their money in the new banks.

I ultimately decided the latter belief took precedence and entered into a contract to develop and present seven-day bank security workshops in south Florida over several years.

Travel to Moscow

In December, 1994, a workshop attendee (a former KBG general) who attended my first bank security workshop invited me to give a presentation on bank security at Russia's first private security seminar to be held in Moscow in January, 1995. I would arrange and pay for my airfare, and sponsors of the seminar would cover all arrangements in Moscow.

As I believed my talks on the need for Russian bank security regulation and depositor insurance was very much needed, I agreed to be a speaker. My topics would focus on FDIC security rules and deposit insurance in the United States. I was told approximately seven hundred attendees were expected at the seminar.

As I prepared for my first visit to Russia, I had some personal concerns. The Russians knew of my former CIA employment since it was public information and noted in my resume. I knew I had to be extremely circumspect while in Moscow to avoid any action that could lead the Russians to conclude I was still an active CIA agent. I did not want to be arrested on an espionage charge.

I arrived at the Moscow airport in mid-January on a very cold day following a recent snow storm. I processed through immigration and customs without incident and was met by an English-speaking gentleman who drove me to the Hotel National where I would be staying for the next week.

The Hotel National is a five-star hotel built in the early 1900s; from my spacious room with many historical furniture pieces, I could see the Kremlin and Red Square. My contact registered me at the hotel and noted that he would meet me in the hotel's front parking lot the next morning at 9:00 am. He explained that we would then proceed to his office where I would meet his boss, the former KBG general.

The seminar proceedings were simultaneously translated into English through headphones so that I and other non-Russian attendees could understand the speakers. Also, whenever I was at the seminar, a personal translator was assigned to me.

The Past Meets the Present

I had several memorable experiences interfacing with former KGB officers during my visit to Russia. One encounter, however, is especially relevant to my conclusions in this book.

Immediately following my presentation on the FDIC, one English-speaking attendee handed me his business card that, in English, identified him as a retired Russian intelligence service employee. He asked: "We cannot find a record of your [CIA] service. When did you serve?" I answered, "In the Far East during the 1950s."

The next morning as I was walking to my chair on the podium, the retired intelligence officer again approached me. He asked if I had served in Tokyo during 1953 and 1954 working for a chief of station that he correctly named. He also correctly identified the years of my CIA tour of duty in Tokyo. I replied affirmatively to his questions.

With this correct Russian confirmation about my undercover assignment to Tokyo, I must conclude the KGB was active in Japan during the time of my deployment to Tokyo.

I do not know where the Soviet KGB intelligence service in Japan was headquartered in the 1950s. However, this Moscow encounter confirms my belief that Soviet intelligence agents were operating in Japan during the time the CIA U-2 project was based in Atsugi, Japan and that the Soviets were aware of Lee Harvey Oswald's Marine Corps assignment to the U.S. Naval Air Station at Atsugi in 1957.

Subsequent Encounters

Following my remarks to the conference, I was taken, with my personal interpreter, to a private room where I met the press. There was immense interest by the media in exploring my remarks in more detail. Later, I was to learn that my speech and comments were reported in the Russian version of the *Wall Street Journal*.

On my last day in Moscow, the former KBG general who had attended my first bank security workshop invited me to visit his Moscow residence. The general and his English-speaking son met me at the Hotel National in a new Mercedes driven by a chauffeur. As we approached the general's grey multi-story apartment building, he remarked: "This is where Khrushchev lived." Yes, the general did indeed impress me that he was a person of influence in the affairs of the former Soviet Union.

We took the elevator to an upper floor and, upon entering the apartment's foyer, the general directed my attention to four crosses placed on the walls near the ceiling. He announced and his son translated to English: "This is where my friend, a Russian priest, has blessed my home." I, of course found it difficult to believe a former Soviet KGB general could also be a Christian in the Russian Orthodox Church.

My Final Bank Security Workshop

In April 1995, following my trip to Moscow, I conducted a final workshop for approximately fifteen Russians at a motel in the West Palm Beach area. The former KGB general who attended my first workshop and who had invited me to Moscow again was in the audience.

On the first day of the workshop, I observed a well-dressed man at the motel's front desk engaging an employee in conversation. I immediately thought this person's demeanor was that of a FBI agent. After his departure, I confirmed with the front desk employee that the gentleman, indeed, did identify himself as an agent of the FBI. I assumed that one or more of the Russians attending the workshop were of interest to the FBI.

Was the general in some manner involved with Russia's newly-created Foreign Intelligence Service, which had replaced the KGB? Since I believe in the old intelligence expression, "once a spy always a spy," I think the answer is yes.

As I look back on my consulting engagement with the Russians, I sincerely hope that my contribution to Russia's emerging banking system provided the fundamental security protocols necessary to prevent criminal activity directed against banks and their customers. The citizens of Russia need to have faith in the integrity of their country's financial system.

I also believe that each of the nearly eighty former Soviet intelligence officers, including the general, who attended my workshops began to learn the process for establishing a cadre of security officers for the emerging Russian banking system and the private security profession.

Has the Russian government put into place the regulations and guidance needed to create fundamental bank security procedures and protocols applicable its financial institutions? Only time will tell.

Final Reflections

I remain optimistic that this historical look at the events surrounding the assassination of President John F. Kennedy will stimulate students of American history to examine the thousands of documents in the Warren Commission's report to conclusively establish what transpired on November 22, 1963.

My research to date formed the theories expressed in this book on the role of Lee Harvey Oswald. But, as I mention in the Preface and Prologue, Jack Ruby, Oswald's assassin, is another strategic but shadowy figure in the story. Previously sealed documents released in 1992 by the Dallas Police Department hold the promise of new details about a possible connection between Oswald and Ruby. Did they know each other and were their actions part of an even wider conspiracy?

That intriguing possibility certainly opens a door for further research.

Endnotes

[1] The Warren Commission, *The Warren Report: The Official Report on the Assassination of President John F. Kennedy*, Associated Press, 1964, p. 12.

[2] Earl Warren et.al., *Report of the President's Commission on the Assassination of President Kennedy*, U.S. Government Printing Office, Washington, D.C., 1964, Chap. 2, pp. 28-29.

[3] Ibid. pp. 42-43.

[4] Ibid. p. 43.

[5] Ibid. p. 58.

[6] Ibid.

[7] Governor Connally, who was also wounded in the shooting, underwent surgery and ultimately recovered from his serious wounds.

[8] *The Warren Report*, pp. 253-268.

[9] After leaving the Dallas Police Department in 1968, Dallas Police Detective Paul Bentley became security director at First National

Bank in Dallas for eleven years. I met him in 1974 when I was ASIS International president and he was ASIS International North Texas Chapter chairman. Unfortunately, I did not discuss the Kennedy assassination with him, and I regret not having done so. Bentley is now deceased; if alive, I believe he would have been a valuable source for my research.

[10] *The Warren Report*, p. iii.

[11] *Report of the President's Commission*, Chap.1, p. 1.

[12] *The Warren Report*, p. v.

[13] President Gerald F. Ford, *President John F. Kennedy Assassination Report of the Warren Commission*, The FlatSigned Press, Nashville, TN, 2004, p xv.

[14] Material in this chapter is based on G. W. Pedlow and D. E. Welzenbach, *The CIA and the U-2 Program 1954-1974*, Central Intelligence Agency, 1974, and *The Warren Report*.

[15] Pedlow and Welzenbach, *The CIA and the U-2 Program 1954-1974*, p. 97.

[16] Material in this chapter is based on Pedlow and Welzenbach, *The CIA and the U-2 Program 1954-1974*; *The Warren Report*; and Francis Gary Powers, *Operation Overflight*, Holt, Rinehart & Winston, 1970.

[17] Powers, *Operation Overflight*, p. 82.

[18] Warren Commission Hearings Volume XVI-XXVI, Exhibit 315. Retrieved March 9, 2013, from http://www.history-matters.com/ archieve/center.

Author's Note:
In 2013, while conducting primary research for this book, I visited the U S. National Archives in College Park, Maryland. While there,

I searched the Warren Commission files and confirmed the existence of Exhibit 315: Lee Harvey Oswald's letter to his brother, Robert, reporting that he saw Francis Gary Powers in Moscow. Because of its major relevance to this manuscript, I ordered and paid for a copy of this exhibit along with many others.

Seven weeks later, I received a CD from the National Archives containing fifteen exhibits. However, the CD did not include Exhibit 315 and omitted two other relevant exhibits.

Subsequently, I sent a certified letter to the National Archives requesting the missing exhibits. No response had been received by this book's publication date.

[19] Powers, *Operation Overflight*, p. 283.

[20] Ibid. p. 307.

[21] Material in this chapter is from the *Report of the President's Commission*.

[22] My research did not disclose a reply to Oswald from the Socialist Party of America.

[23] *Report of the President's Commission*, App. 13, p. 681.

[24] See Postscript where I discuss my Moscow experiences in 1995.

[25] *Report of the President's Commission*, App. 15, pp. 747-748.

[26] Francis Gary Powers, *Operation Overflight*, pp. 357-358.

[27] My research in this chapter is from the *Report of the President's Commission*.

[28] Warren Commission Hearings Volume XVI-XXVI, Exhibit 244.

[29] Emphasis added by author.

[30] Warren Commission Hearings Volume XVI-XXVI, Exhibit 796.

[31] My research in this chapter is from the *Report of the President's Commission*.

[32] Warren Commission Hearings Volume XVI-XXVI, Exhibit 245.

[33] *Report of the President's Commission*, App. 15, pp. 753-754.

[34] My research in this chapter is from the *Report of the President's Commission*.

[35] Warren Commission Hearings Volume XVI-XXVI, Exhibit 1.

[36] *Report of the President's Commission*, Chap. 7, p. 405.

[37] Ibid. Chap. 2, p. 40.

[38] Ibid. Chap. 6, p. 299.

[39] Ibid.

[40] Warren Commission Hearings Volume XVI-XXVI, Exhibit 2763.

[41] *Report of the President's Commission*, Chap. 6, p. 309.

[42] Ibid. pp. 309-310.

[43] Ibid. Chap. 7, pp. 423-424.

[44] Ibid. Chap. 6, p. 254.

[45] Ibid. p. 255.

[46] Ibid. p. 256.

[47] Ibid. Chap.1, p. 21.

[48] Vladislov Zubok, "Atomic Espionage and its Soviet Witnesses," *Cold War International History Project Bulletin*, Woodrow Wilson International Center for Scholars, Issue 4, Fall 1994, p. 50.

[49] Ibid.

[50] Inaugural Address, January 20, 1961, John F. Kennedy Presidential Library and Museum, Boston, MA.

Inserts

Insert 1: President Kennedy's motorcade in Dallas before and immediately after the shooting.

Insert 2: The rifle Oswald used to kill President Kennedy.

Insert 3: Oswald's letter to the Socialist Party of America.

Insert 4: Oswald's U.S. passport.

Insert 5: River in Minsk seen from Oswald's apartment.

Insert 6: Oswald's application for P. O. Box 30061.

Insert 7: Oswald with his wife, Marina, in Minsk.

Insert 8: *Dallas Times Herald* newspaper article dated September 16, 1963.

Insert 9: Oswald's Mexican tourist card application.

Insert 10: Oswald's letter to the Soviet Embassy in Washington, D.C., following his return from Mexico in 1963.

References

Earl Warren et.al., *Report of the President's Commission on the Assassination of President Kennedy*, U.S. Government Printing Office, Washington, D.C., 1964.

    Chapter1: Summary and Conclusions
    Chapter 2: The Assassination
    Chapter 4: The Assassin
    Chapter 5: Detention and Death of Oswald
    Chapter 6: Investigation of Possible Conspiracy
    Chapter 7: Lee Harvey Oswald: Background and Possible Motives
    Appendix 11: Reports Relating to the Interrogation of Lee Harvey Oswald at the Dallas Police Department
    Appendix 12: Speculations and Rumors
    Appendix 13: Biography of Lee Harvey Oswald
    Appendix 15: Transactions Between Lee Harvey Oswald and Marina Oswald and the U.S. Department of State and the Immigration and Naturalization Ser vice, U.S. Department of Justice

Francis Gary Powers, *Operation Overflight*, Holt, Rinehart & Winston, 1970.

Gerald F. Ford, *President John F. Kennedy: Assassination Report of the Warren Commission*, The FlatSigned Press, Nashville, TN, 2004.

G.W. Pedlow and D.E. Weizenbach, *The CIA and the U-2, 1954-1974*, Central Intelligence Agency, 1974.

John F. Kennedy Presidential Library and Museum, Boston, MA.

State of Louisiana v. *Clay L. Shaw*. 198-059 1426 (30) Section "C." (1969). Excerpt from the testimony of Marina Oswald Porter taken in open court on February 21, 1969.

Vladislov Zubok, "Atomic Espionage and its Soviet Witnesses," *Cold War International History Project Bulletin*, Woodrow Wilson International Center for Scholars, Issue 4, Fall 1994, p. 50.

The Warren Commission, *The Warren Report: The Official Report on the Assassination of President John F. Kennedy*, Associated Press, 1964.

Warren Commission Hearings and Exhibits, *Final Report of the President's Commission on the Assassination of President John F. Kennedy*, U.S. Government Printing Office, Washington, D.C., 1964.

Warren Commission Hearings Volume XVI-XXVI. Retrieved March 9, 2013, from http://www.history-matters.com/archieve/center.

Index

Walker assassination attempt, 48–49, 60
Oswald, Marina
    arrival in U.S., 43–44, 64–65
    marriage of, 39–40, *40*
    as post office box recipient, 38, *38,* 47
    testimony given by, 33, 51, 54, 56, 57
    Walker assassination attempt, knowledge of, 48–49
Oswald, Robert, iv, 21, 44–45, 46

P
Paine, Ruth, 38, 47, 54
Parkland Memorial Hospital, 4
Pett, Saul, 12
Pool, Joe, 49, 51
Postal Inspection Service, U.S., 10–11, 38
Powers, Francis Gary, iv–v, 16, 18, 19–22, 26, 44–45
A Presidential Legacy and the Warren Commission (Ford), 12
Presidential motorcade, 1–3, *2*
Presidential Protective Branch of Secret Service, 10
President's Commission on the Assassination of President John F.
    Kennedy. *See* Warren Commission
President's Science Advisory Committee (PSAC), 17–18
Prusakova, Marina. *See* Oswald, Marina
Putin, Vladimir, i

R
Radar detection, 16, 25–26
Rifle used in JFK assassination, *7*
Ruby, Jack, i, 71
Rusk, Dean, 57, 61
Russell, Richard, 11

S
Secret Service, U.S., iii, 1, 3, 10
Setyayec, Lev, 32
Shirokova, Rima, 31–32

W

Walker, Edwin, 48–49, 60

Warrantless searches, 10

Warren, Earl, 11

Warren Commission

    on character of Oswald, 49, 60

    criticisms of, 65

    on firing location, iv

    investigative activities of, 9, 11–12

    on letter to Soviet Embassy written by Oswald, 53–54, 56

    on Marine Corps service of Oswald, 23, 27, 30

    on marriage of Oswald, 39

    on Mexico visit of Oswald, 51, 56–57

    on motives for killing JFK, 60–61

    on post office boxes, 37–38

    rejection of conspiracy theories, i

    on Soviet defection of Oswald, 26, 30, 32, 60

    on Soviet involvement in assassination, 60–61

    on U-2 program, 15

The Warren Report: The Official Report on the Assassination of President Kennedy (Pett), 12

CPSIA information can be obtained at www.ICGtesting.com
Printed in the USA
LVOW12s2045311013

359489LV00001B/3/P